The incarnation is the most accurate and articulate translation.

Any sincere student of classical music would sensitively seek to capture and interpret the piece, so as not to distract from the original sound of the composition.

To form a conclusion in the study of our origin would involve a peering over the Creator's shoulder as it were, in order to gaze through his eyes and marvel at his anticipation. His invisible image and likeness is about to be unveiled in human form!

The incarnation celebrates the fact that the destiny of the Word was not the page but tangible human life! The word of truth preserves God's original idea in the resonance of our hearts.

2 Corinthians 3:2 Instead of an impressive certificate framed on my wall I have you framed in my heart! You are our Epistle written within us, an open letter speaking a global language; one that everyone can [1]read and recognize as their mother tongue! (The word [1]anaginosko, from ana, upward and ginosko, to know upward; thus to draw knowledge from a higher reference; from above; to recognize; to read with recognition.)

2 Corinthians 3:3 The fact that you are a Christ-Epistle shines as bright as day! This is what our ministry is all about. The Spirit of God is the living ink. Every trace of the Spirit's influence on the heart is what gives permanence to this conversation. We are not talking law-language here; this is more dynamic and permanent than letters chiselled in stone. This conversation is embroidered in your inner consciousness. (It is the life of your design that grace echoes within you!)

Behold how beautiful
how valuable
how loved
you are!

John's Beautiful Gospel

Sixty years after he last saw Jesus in the flesh, John, now in his nineties, reflects on the mystery that was revealed in him, which transformed his life from an illiterate fisherman to a saint.

Editing preparation for printing: Sean Osmond

Mirror Word Logo by: Wilna Furstenburg

Cover Design by: Sean Osmond

Published by Mirror Word Publishing

Should you wish to order printed copies in bulk, [2 or more] pls contact us at info@mirrorword.net

Contact us if you wish to help sponsor Mirror Bibles in Spanish, Shona or Xhosa.

Highly recommended books by the same author: Divine Embrace, God Believes in You, The Logic of His Love.

Children's books: The Eagle Story, by Lydia and Francois du Toit, illustrated by Carla Krige

Stella's Secret by Lydia du Toit and illustrated by Wendy Francisco. Also in German.

Lydia has also released 2 more beautiful children's stories, The Little Bear and The Mirror and her latest book, Kaa!

The Mirror Bible, Divine Embrace God Believes in You and The Logic of His Love are also available on Kindle. The new updated Mirror Bible App is avaiable on our website

www.mirrorword.net

Subscribe to Francois facebook updates http://www.facebook.com/francois.toit

The Mirror Translation fb group http://www.facebook.com/groups/179109018883718/

ISBN 978-0-9922303-2-6

THE MIRROR STUDY BIBLE

The Mirror Study Bible is a paraphrased translation from the Greek text. While strictly following the literal meaning of the original, sentences have been constructed so that the larger meaning is continually emphasized by means of an expanded text.

Some clarifying notes are included in italics. This is a paraphrased study rather than a literal translation. While the detailed shades of meaning of every Greek word and its components have been closely studied, this is done taking into account the consistent context of the entire chapter within the wider epistle, and bearing in mind that Jesus is what the Scriptures are all about and humankind is what Jesus is all about.

To assist the reader in their study, I have numerically superscripted the Greek word and corresponded it with the closest English word in the italicized commentary that follows. This is to create a direct comparison of words between the two languages.

I translated several Pauline epistles in the eighties but these were never published. In 2007 I started with the Mirror Translation.

This is an ongoing process and will eventually include the entire New Testament

as well as select portions of the Old Testament.

The Ninth edition - is a 944 page book which is also available on Kindle or as an App in Android as well as in Apple.

The following individual books are also separately available,

Revelation, Romans, Hebrews, Philippians and Vol 1 and Vol 2 of three Volumes of Luke (8 Chapters each)

In the Mirror,
Bible language becomes heart to heart
whispers of grace!

Jesus Christ, the Incarnation, mankind's co-inclusion,
co-crucifixion, co-resurrection and co-seatedness in him, is
the only valid context and theme of Scripture.

This is the good of the Good News!

Jesus exhibits the Father and the Holy Spirit in one man,

in action!

Jesus is God's language and message to mankind.

To add anything to his completed work in revealing and
redeeming the image of God in human form,

or take anything away from what God spoke to us in him,

is to depart from the essence of the Gospel.

There is no perfect translation,

there is only a perfect Word: the Logic of God.

The Bible is all about Jesus.

What makes the book irresistibly relevant, is the fact that

Jesus is all about you!

God has found a face in you that portrays him

more beautifully than the best theology!

Your features, your touch, the cadence of your voice,

the compassion in your gaze, the lines of your smile,

the warmth of your person and presence unveil him!

INDEX

Reflecting on any translation of Scripture gives one the opportunity to hear our Maker's voice and thoughts, filtered through the interpretation and language of the translator(s). In this fresh Paraphrase, Francois du Toit has opened the curtain for readers of any age, culture or language to enjoy amazing insights into the heartbeat of *Agape* - where everyone feels equally loved, included and valued in the eyes of the Father - and fully redeemed in the union we come from! The Mirror underlines the fact that we did not merely begin in our mother's womb; we are the invention and idea of God!

To have this work now also available in Xhosa will mark a new era for young and old to rediscover the Bible afresh.

Archbishop **DESMOND TUTU** - *Legacy Foundation*

The Mirror Bible is a transforming paraphrased translation that is simplistic, accurate, detailed and comprehensive, captivating and at the same time exuding intriguing spiritual revelation; it is divinely insightful and contemporary.

It's a must read, a befitting guide and manual for all age groups for; Bible study, meditation, devotion, worship, teaching, instruction and scholarship.

Jesus Christ is the epicenter of the entire text.

Believers will not miss the centrality of the translation as there is a finite and delicate thread directing to the revealing and redeeming Christ.

Unbelievers will derive unrivaled comfort from the text as they get captivated by the reality and close proximity of Christ.

This is definitely a life giving and transforming translation. I am humbly convinced that Francois is chosen by God to serve this generation and the next with undiluted truth in the midst of incomprehensible compromises of worldly, heretical and traditional, doctrinal interpretations and practices (religion) that have diverted us from the truth.

The Mirror Bible is a welcome revelatory and revolutionary development that is divinely sanctioned, inspired and directed. This translation is by no doubt a compelling grounding expository of our century.

To God be the Glory.

Rev. **ANOUYA ANDREW MUCHECHETERE**, *MBA, MA,*

Former Secretary General of the Evangelical Fellowship of Zimbabwe (EFZ).

The mystery concerning God's Own action in Christ, balanced with the nature and necessity of our human response has defined my personal journey for many years.
When I was introduced to Francois du Toit and the Mirror Bible, much of that mystery were resolved. Often, I found myself 'gasping for breath' as some new aspect of the mystery of Christ and His Kingdom emerged with startling clarity.
Francois' love for the text, his sheer exegetical courage and his astonishing ability to express essential biblical presuppositions in the intimate Love language of God, has opened for Judith and me a renewed and transformative biblical understanding.

BOB and **JUDITH MUMFORD** - www.lifechangers.org

The Mirror Translation is astonishingly beautiful. The union theme is outstanding.
The early followers of Jesus knew that he was the center of all creation, the plan from the beginning, the alpha and the omega, the author and finisher of faith. They wrestled deeply with these questions and the staggering implications of Jesus's very identity. They handed down clear and powerful and very relevant insights and answers. Francois has met the Jesus of the Apostles, and through his wrestling with their light, is providing for us all a paraphrase of their work that is as thrilling as it is beautiful and true.
My imagination ignites reading the Mirror Bible. What a beautiful, breathtaking translation. This is brilliant, and destined to relieve and liberate many. You sing the Father's heart, my brother. May the Holy Spirit continue to use the Mirror to reveal Jesus and his Father and us all around this world! I love it.

DR. C. BAXTER KRUGER *Author of "The Great Dance" and "The Shack Revisited"*

In a world where Bible translations and paraphrases are ubiquitous, *The Mirror Study Bible* is uniquely beautiful and helpful! Submitted to the original texts and the abiding guidance of the Holy Spirit, Francois du Toit carefully and meticulously opens and explores the treasures of Scripture. Not only does it satisfy the demands of the intellect, but it overwhelms the heart.

WM PAUL YOUNG - *Author of The Shack*

I have been asked at times why God didn't make the Bible easier to understand. If He is able to inspire the writings of Scripture, couldn't He provide a key for unlocking its treasures for us? *The Mirror Translation* you hold in your hand opens the treasure-chest of understanding with that Key. The key to properly understanding the Bible is Jesus Christ. He is the source and subject of its pages. For years I have been asked why there isn't a Bible translation that presents the Scriptures from a pure grace orientation. It is a great encouragement to know that the Mirror Bible is just that. Drawing not only from the literal meaning, but also the historical nuances of the Greek language, Francois Du Toit presents this translation in a way that will enrich your love for our Triune God and ground you in the grace expressed to us all through Jesus Christ. This is a translation you will read again and again. It is one you will share with your friends.

DR. STEVE McVEY - *Founder of Grace Walk Ministries, Florida*

The Bible is God's amazing conversation with us. Here we engage with God's words that crescendo in the revelation of his Son, Jesus Christ. The greatest joy is to realize that you as an individual are included in this conversation.

This translation is in all probability one of the greatest contributions in the last few years to the broader church. It is imperative that every Christ follower discovers their true identity mirrored in Jesus. The most liberating revelation is the fact that we have not only died together with Him, but that we were also raised with Him in resurrection life. Then to grasp that we are seated with Him in heavenly places, where we may now live our daily lives from a position of significance and influence within this world. The premise of the Good News of the Gospel is that we are not required to strive to attain something through personal achievement, but rather to discover who we already are and what we already have in Christ, as revealed in the glorious Scriptures.

May The Mirror Translation impact your life as much as it has mine, and may it facilitate your spiritual journey to truly relocate your mind, living from the new vantage point of this glorious life in Christ.

ALAN Platt - *Visionary leader of **Doxa Deo** International*

My philosophy in doing the Mirror Bible is reflected in the following example:

I do not read music, but have often witnessed our son, Stefan, approach a new piece on the piano.

His eyes see so much more than mere marks scribbled on a page;

he hears the music.

His trained mind engages even the subtleties and the nuances of the original composition, and is able to repeat the authentic sound,

knowing that the destiny of the music would never be reduced to the page;

but is always in the next moment,

where the same intended beauty is heard, and repeated again!

The best translation would always be the incarnation!

I so value the enormity of the revelation of the incarnation.

Yet, before flesh, the Word was προς

face to face with God!

And fragile text

scribbled through the ages in memoirs of stone, parchment and papyrus pages

carrying eternity in thought

and continues to translate faith

to faith!

Now we have the same spirit of faith as he encountered when he wrote...

"I believe

and so I speak!"

Conversation ignites!

Did not our hearts burn within our being when He spoke familiar text of ancient times, in the voices of Moses and the prophets and David and Abraham,

who saw his day

and announced its dawn in our hearts!

The mystery that was hidden for ages and generations

is now revealed!

In dealing daily with ancient text,

rediscovering thoughts buried in time, I am often overwhelmed and awed at the magnificence of eternity captured in little time capsules,

opening vistas of beauty beyond our imagination -

face to face with the same face to faceness of the Logos

and God

and us - conceived in their dream!

And irresistibly intrigued by the invitation to come and drink -

to taste and see -

from the source -

and to hear a saint reminiscing and reminding himself of the utterance of another earth dweller-brother, David, who wrote a song 3000 years ago,

"Return to your rest oh my soul!

For the Lord has dealt bountifully with you!

I believe and so I speak!"

And with fresh wounds bleeding from the many angry blows he was dealt with, Paul echoes,

"We have the same spirit of faith as he had who wrote, 'I believe and so I speak!' We too believe and so we speak!"

Let's celebrate the "sameness" of Jesus

yesterday - yes, as far as history and beyond time can go -

and today! This very finite, fragile moment -

plus the infinite future!

Inexhaustible, beyond boundaries and the confines of space and time!

JOHN'S ENCOUNTER OF JESUS

Sixty years after he last saw Jesus in the flesh, John, now in his nineties, reflects on the mystery that was revealed which transformed his life from an illiterate fisherman to a saint. He spent most of the latter part of his life (about 30 years) living in Asia Minor and more specifically at Ephesus; much of Paul's emphasis in teaching therefore reflects in John's writing. This he did both from Ephesus as well as from the Isle of Patmos where he spent some years in exile. (*Compare Colossians 1:15-17, John 1:1-3,16-17, 1 John 5:20, "He has given us understanding to know him who is true and we are in him who is true!"*)

None of the other disciples better captured the conclusion of the mission of Christ than John, *"In that day you will know that we are in seamless union with one another! I am in my Father, you are in me and I am in you!" John 14:20*

He has no desire to outwit the others in giving an even more accurate historic account of Christ! The life that was manifest within his sacred gaze and now tangible embrace is a fellowship of the highest order! He must write; he must extend this reality to his immediate audience as well as the next generations! "I am writing this to complete your joy!" 1 John 1:4

Unlike Matthew and Luke who wrote 30 years prior to him, John did not bother to locate Jesus in the setting of his natural lineage. Instead he declares, "In the beginning was the Word!" Before history was ever recorded the Word was!

Mankind pre-existed in the Logic of God! He understands that the Word was both the eternal source and destiny of all things and that nothing could ever reduce or confine the Word to an isolated island experience, neither could the Word be trapped in human doctrine or tradition. No inferior translation or interpretation could compromise God's original intent. The authentic integrity of God's thought would forever be preserved and celebrated in the incarnation; human life would be the uninterrupted future of the Word.

Notice how often John uses the word, *egeneto*, from **ginomai**, meaning birth or origin in the first chapter: "In the beginning was the Word, and the Word was face to face towards God, and the Word was God. All things came into being (**ginomai**, *from* **genos**, *to give birth to*) through him; and nothing has any authentic existence outside of their origin (*ginomai*) in him.

11

In him was life and the life was the light of men. The light shone in the darkness, and the darkness could not comprehend it *(kata+lambano, to seize upon, to grasp)*. The true light that enlightens everyone has come into the world. The world was made *(ginomai)* through him, yet the world knew him not; he came to his own, and his own received him not *(para+lambano, to grasp, associate with)*.

But in everyone who by faith comprehends him to be their true origin *(lambano, comprehend, grasp, identify with)*, in them he sanctions the integrity of their sonship *(didomi, in this case to give something to someone that already belongs to them, thus to return)*, the fact that they already are his own, born from above, they have their beginning and their being in him *(eksousia, integrity, legality, authority, legal grounds)*! Jesus has come to reveal mankind's true sonship; he vindicated our origin and design.

"And the Word became *(ginomai)* flesh and now tabernacles in *(en)* us!" Not 'amongst us' as many translations would suggest! John 1:1-14.

1 John 2:7 My beloved family, I know that the words I write to you here may not immediately remind you of the [1]precepts of Moses; this does not mean that it is a new [1]doctrine, it is the ancient [1]conversation that [2]echoes God's voice prophetically! It is indeed the very [1]conclusion of the word, which you have heard from the beginning! *(The word [1]entole is often translated commandment or precept; this word has two components: en, in and telos, from tello, to set out for a definite point or goal; properly the point aimed at as a limit, that is, by implication, the conclusion of an act or state, the result; the ultimate or prophetic purpose. Strong's 5056. The word, [2]echo, to hold, like sound is held in an echo; to resonate.)*

1 John 2:8 And yet it is a glorious [1]new [2]message that I am writing to you! You may ask, "How can that which is old, also be new?" Herein is the secret of its newness: **whatever is true of Jesus is equally true of you!** The days of the [3]dominance of darkness as a reference to human life, are over! The true light surely shines with [4]bold certainty and illuminates your life, as it is unveiled in Christ. *(The word [1]kainos means, fresh, recent, unused, unworn, of a new kind, unprecedented, novel, uncommon. The freshness of this encounter is celebrated in a fellowship of exactly the*

same oneness enjoyed between the Father and the Son! Again the word
²*entole* is used, precept or teaching. The word ³*parago* from para, close
proximity and *agoo*, to lead; thus darkness will no longer lead you
into its sway. The word ⁴*ede*, even now: - already, by this time; from *ē*
[pronounced, **ay**] an adverb of confirmation; assuredly: - surely; and
dē [pronounced, **day**] which is a particle of emphasis or explicitness;
now, then, etc.: - also, and, doubtless, now, therefore.)

As he is so are we in this world! 1 John 4:17.

In him we discover our genesis in God, beyond our natural
conception! This is not about our blood lineage or whether
we were a wanted- or unwanted-child; this is about our God-
begotteness. John 1:13. We are his dream come true and not the
invention of our parents. You are indeed the greatest idea that
God has ever had! God said to Jeremiah, "I knew you before I
formed you in your mother's womb." *(See Jeremiah 1:5; 29:11
& John 3:2-7)* The eternal, invisible Word, the Spirit-thought of
God's face to face union, became flesh (**ginomai**, *be born*). James
says: "Of his own will he brought us forth by the word of truth
... if anyone hears this word, he sees the face of his birth as in
a mirror." James 1:17, 18, 23 RSV. Now we may know even as
we have always been known. 1 Corinthians 13:12.

God never compromised his original thought. "The word
became flesh and took up residence *(tabernacled)* in us, and
we gazed with wonder and amazement upon the mystery of
our inclusion in him (**theaomai**, *to gaze upon, to perceive*). We
saw his glory (**doxa**, *the display of his opinion*); the glory as of
the original, authentic begotten of the Father, full of grace and
truth." *(The original mind, or opinion of God, preserved and now
revealed in Christ. He is both the "only begotten," **monogenes**, as in
the authentic original mold, as well as the first born from the dead.
Colossians 1:18, 1Peter 1:3.)*

He is the revelation of our completeness. "Of his fullness have
we all received, grace mirrored in grace" (**garin anti garitos**).
"For the law was given through Moses, grace and truth came
through Jesus Christ. He who is in the bosom of the Father,
the only *(original, authentic)* begotten of the Father, he is our
guide who accurately declares and interprets the invisible
God within us." John 1:1-5, 9-14,16-18.

1 John 1:1 The Logos is the source; everything commences in
him. The initial reports concerning him that have reached our

ears, and which we indeed bore witness to with our own eyes - to the point that we became irresistibly attracted - now captivates our gaze. In him we witnessed tangible life in its most articulate form. *(To touch, **psallo**, to touch the string of a musical instrument; thus to be deeply touched as in resonance.)*

1 John 1:2 The same life that was face to face with the Father from the beginning, has now dawned on us! The infinite life of the Father became visible before our eyes in a human person! *(In the beginning "was" the Word; **eimi**, timeless existence, "I am". The preposition **pros** says so much more than 'with,' it suggests towards; face to face. See John 1:1&2. Also John 1:14 "Suddenly the invisible eternal Word takes on visible form! The Incarnation! In him, and now confirmed in us! The most accurate tangible display of God's eternal thought finds expression in human life! The Word became a human being; we are his address; he resides in us! He captivates our gaze! The glory we see there is not a religious replica; he is the authentic begotten Son. The glory [that Adam lost sight of] is now fully unveiled! Only grace can communicate truth in such complete context!" Also John 1:18 "Until this moment God remained invisible; now the authentic begotten Son, the blueprint of mankind's design who represents the innermost being of God, the Son who is in the bosom of the Father, brings him into full view! He is the official authority qualified to announce God! He is our guide who accurately declares and interprets the invisible God within us.")*

1 John 1:3 We include you in this conversation; you are the immediate audience of the logic of God! This is the Word that always was; we saw him incarnate and witnessed his language as defining our lives. In the incarnation Jesus includes mankind in the eternal friendship of the Father and the Son! This life now finds expression in an unreserved union. *(We do not invent fellowship; we are invited into the fellowship of the Father and the Son!)*

1 John 1:4 What we enjoy equally belongs to you! I am writing this for your reference, so that joy may be yours in its most complete measure. *(In all these years since the ascension of Jesus, John, now ninety years old, continues to enjoy unhindered friendship with God and desires to extend this same fellowship to everyone through this writing.)*

1 John 1:5 My conversation with you flows from the same source which illuminates this fellowship of union with the Father and the Son. This, then, is the essence of the message: God is radiant

light and in him there exists not even a trace of obscurity or darkness at all. *(See James 1:17, "Without exception God's gifts are only good, their perfection cannot be improved upon. They come from above, [where we originate from] proceeding like light rays from the source, the Father of lights, with whom there is no distortion or even a shadow of shifting to obstruct or intercept the light; no hint of a hidden agenda. The word, anouthen, means, from above. John 3:3, 13. Mankind is not the product of their mother's womb; man began in God.")*

John 3:7 Don't be so surprised when I say to you'manity' *(plural!)* You couldn't get here in the flesh unless you got here from above! *(See John 1:13 These are the ones who discover their genesis in God beyond their natural conception! This is not about our blood lineage or whether we were a wanted or an unwanted child - this is about our God-begotteness; we are his dream come true! We are not the invention of our parents! [You are the greatest idea God has ever had!])*

John 3:13 No one can fully engage in heaven's perspective, unless one's heavenly origin is realized! The Son of man declares mankind's co-genesis from above!

Another pivotal reference John records is when Jesus defended his message when he declared, to the disgust of the religious leaders, "My Father and I are one!" *(John 10:30)* Jesus then quoted Psalm 82:6, "I say you are gods, sons of the Most High, all of you!"

In John 14:20 Jesus declares the conclusion of his mission where in his death and resurrection every possible definition of separation will be cancelled: "In that day you will know that we are in seamless union with one another! I am in my Father, you are in me and I am in you!" *(The incarnation does not divide the Trinity; the incarnation celebrates the redeemed inclusion of humanity! Picture four circles with the one fitting into the other - The outer circle is the Father, then Jesus in the Father, then us in Jesus and the Holy Spirit in us! This spells inseparable, intimate oneness! Note that it is not our knowing that positions Jesus in the Father or us in them or the Spirit of Christ in us! Our knowing simply awakens us to the reality of our redeemed oneness! Gold does not become gold when it is discovered but it certainly becomes currency!)*

1:1 To go back to the very ¹beginning, is to find the ²Word already ³present there; ⁴face to face with God. The Word is ³I am; God's ²eloquence echoes and ⁴concludes in him. The Word equals God. *(In the beginning, ¹arche, to be first in order, time, place or rank. The Word, ²logos, was "with" God; here and again in verse 2 John uses the Greek preposition ⁴pros, towards; face-to-face.*

Three times in this sentence John uses the Active Indicative Imperfect form of the verb ³eimi, namely aen [ἦν] to continue to be, [in the beginning 'was' the Word etc...] which conveys no idea of origin for God or for the Logos, but simply continuous existence, "I am." Quite a different verb egeneto, "became," appears in John 1:14 for the beginning of the Incarnation of the Logos. The Word 'became' flesh. The incarnation is not the origin of Jesus. See the distinction sharply drawn in John 8:58, "before Abraham was [born, genesthai from ginomai] I am." The word eimi, I am; the essence of being, suggesting timeless existence. See my commentary note on 1 Pet 1:16)

1:2 **The beginning mirrors the Word face to face with God.** *(Nothing that is witnessed in the Word distracts from who God is. "If you have seen me, you have seen the Father." [John 14:9] The Word that was from the beginning was not yet written nor spoken; it was simply face to face with God! The beginning declares the destiny of the Word, it would always only be who God is and conclude in God.)*

1:3 **The Logos is the source; everything commences in him. He remains the exclusive Parent reference to their existence. There is nothing original, except the Word! The Logic of God defines the only possible place where mankind can trace their origin.** *(All things were made by him; and without him was not any thing made that was made. KJV See Colossians 1:16.)*

1:4 **His life is the light that defines our lives.** *(In his life we discover the light of life.)*

1:5 **The darkness was pierced and could not comprehend or diminish this light.** *(Darkness represents mankind's ignorance of their redeemed identity and innocence [Isa 9:2-4, Isa 60:1-3, Eph 4:18, Col 1:13-15].)*

1:6 **Then there was this man John** *(Jesus' cousin)* **commissioned by God;**

1:7 **his mission was to draw attention to the light of their lives so that what they witnessed in him would cause them to believe** *(in their original life redeemed again).*

1:8 His ministry was not to distract from the light, as if he himself was the light but rather to point out the light Source.

1:9 A new day for mankind has come. The authentic light of life that illuminates everyone was about to dawn in the world! *(This day would begin our calendar and record the fact that human history would forever be divided into before and after Christ. The incarnation would make the image of God visible in human form. In him who is the blueprint of our lives there is more than enough light to displace the darkness in every human life. He is the true light that enlightens everyone! [Col 1:15; 2:9, 10; 2 Cor 4:6])*

1:10 Although no one took any notice of him, he was no stranger to the world; he always was there and is himself the author of all things.

1:11 It was not as though he arrived on a foreign planet; he came to his own, yet his own did not ¹recognize him. *(The Jews should have been the first to recognize him! Revelation 19:12. Also Ps 24:1, "The earth is the Lord's and the fullness thereof, the world and those who dwell in it [RSV]." The word, ¹paralambano, comes from para, a preposition indicating close proximity, a thing proceeding from a sphere of influence, with a suggestion of union of place of residence, to have sprung from its author and giver, originating from, denoting the point from which an action originates, intimate connection; and lambano, to comprehend, grasp, to identify with.)*

1:12 Everyone who ¹realizes their association in him, ⁶convinced that he is their ²original life and that ⁷his name defines them, God ⁵gives the assurance that they are indeed his ⁴offspring, ²begotten of him; he ³sanctions the legitimacy of their sonship. *(The word often translated, to receive, ¹lambano, means to take in hand, to comprehend, to grasp, to identify with. This word suggests that even though he came to his own, there are those who do not ¹identify with their true ²origin revealed in him, and like the many Pharisees they behave like children of a foreign father, the father of lies [John 8: 44]. Neither God's legitimate fatherhood, nor his ownership is in question; mankind's indifference to their true ²origin is the problem. This is what the Gospel addresses with utmost clarity in the person of Jesus Christ. Jesus has come to introduce the individual to themselves again; mankind has forgotten what manner of person they are by design! [James 1:24, Deuteronomy 32:18, Psalm 22:27]*

The word, ²genesthai, from ginomai, means to generate; to become; John employs this verb in the Aorist Infinitive tense, which indicates *prior completion of an action in relationship to a point in time. Greek Infinitives could have either a present or Aorist form. The contrast between the two forms has more to do with aspect than with time. The Present Infinitive is used to express progressive or imperfective aspect. It pictures the action expressed by the verb as being in progress. The Aorist Infinitive however does not express progressive aspect. It presents the action expressed by the verb as a completed unit with a beginning and end. This is an important point since many translations of this verse suggests that God's ability to make us his sons can only be in response to something we must first do in order to trigger God into action! Our grasping [**lambano**] is simply the awakening to the fact that our genesis is already completed in the **Logos**. [See John 1:3] The **Logos** is the source; everything commences in him. He remains the exclusive Parent reference to their genesis. There is nothing original, except the Word. We are his offspring. [see also Acts 17:28]. "He has come to give us understanding to know him who is true and to realize that we are in him who is true." [1 John 5:20]*

*The word, ³**exousia**, often translated "power;" as in, he gave "power" to ²become children of God, is a compound word; from **ek**, always denoting origin or source and **eimi**, I am; thus, out of I am! This gives ³legitimacy and authority to our sonship; ⁴**teknon**, translated as offspring, child.*

*"He has given," ⁵**didomi**, in this case to give something to someone that already belongs to them; thus, to return. The fact that they already are his own, born from above and that they have their ²beginning and their being in him is now confirmed in their realizing it! Convinced, ⁶**pisteo**; ⁷his name **onoma**, is mankind's family name. [see Eph 3:15].*

"He made to be their true selves, their child-of-God selves." — The Message)

1:13 These are the ones who discover their genesis in God, beyond their natural conception! This is not about our blood lineage or whether we were a wanted- or unwanted-child; this is about our God-begotteness. We are his dream come true and not the invention of our parents. You are indeed the greatest idea that God has ever had! *(See Jeremiah 1:5; 29:11 & John 3:2-7)*

1:14 Suddenly the invisible, eternal Word takes on ¹visible form - the Incarnation, on display in a flesh and blood Person, as in a mirror! In him, and now confirmed in us!

The most accurate tangible exhibit of God's eternal thought finds expression in human life! The Word became a human being; we are his address; he resides in us! He [2]captivates our gaze! The glory we see there is not a religious replica; he is the [3]authentic begotten Son. The [4]glory *(that we lost in Adam)* returns in fullness! Only [5]grace can communicate truth in such complete context! *(In him we discover that we are not here by chance or accident or by the desire of an earthly parent, neither are we the product of a mere physical conception; we exist by the expression of God's desire to reveal himself in the flesh. His eternal invisible Word, his Spirit-thought, [1]became flesh, [1]ginomai, as in be born and [2]theaomai, meaning to gaze upon, to perceive. We saw his glory, [4]doxa, the display of his opinion, the glory as of the original, authentic begotten of the Father, full of grace and truth. He is the "only begotten," [3]monogenes; begotten only by the Father and not of the flesh; in him we recognize our true beginning, as in the authentic original mold. He is also the "first born from the dead", declaring our new birth. [Colossians 1:18, 1 Peter 1:3]. He is the revelation of our completeness.*

And out of [ek] his fullness have we all received! The preposition, ek always points to source/origin. Grace mirrored in grace, [5]garin anti garitos. For the law was given through Moses, grace and truth came through Jesus Christ. He who is in the bosom of the Father, the only original, authentic begotten of the Father; he is our guide who accurately declares and interprets the invisible God within us. Interesting that the revelation of the Incarnation in verse 14 doesn't follow verse 2 or 3, but verse 12 and 13! Genesis 1:26 is redeemed! See 2 Corinthians 3:17,18.)

1:15 John the Baptist raised his voice to announce emphatically that Jesus was what his ministry and prophetic message were all about. He declared that Jesus, though younger than him, since he [1]witnessed his [2]birth, ranks above him in prominence and in his Messianic mission - because in his I-am-ness, he always [3]was pre-eminent. *(He was [2]born [2]in front of my eyes - I witnessed his birth, meaning he is younger than I; [1]emprosthen mou [2]gegonen [from ginomai] oti protos mou [3]ean [eimi] - but he [3]was before I was [2]born - Later Jesus reminds us that before Abraham was born, [ginomai] I am! [eimi]")*

1:16 He is the [1]source of our completeness. Everyone may now realize their own completeness as evidenced in him. This is

[2]**grace mirrored in grace!** *(It reminds of Col 2:9,10 The fullness of the Godhead embodied in Christ, reflects our own completeness! Out of [[1]ek] his fullness have we all received! The preposition, **ek** always points to source/origin. His fullness is the source of all that grace communicates as our portion. Grace mirrored in grace - [2]**garin anti garitos**. The word **anti** means over against - thus, mirrored in.)*

1:17 The law was given through Moses; grace and truth have their genesis in Jesus Christ. Against the stark backdrop of the law, with Moses representing the condemned state of mankind, Jesus Christ unveils grace and truth! *(Moses represents the system of performance as basis to one's standing before God; Jesus Christ is incarnate grace and truth! He is the life of our design on display in human form, as in a mirror.)*

1:18 Until this moment God remained invisible; now the [1]authentic, incarnate begotten Son, the blueprint of our design who represents the innermost being of God, the Son who is in the bosom of the Father, brings him into full view! He is the [2]official authority qualified to announce God! He is our guide who accurately declares and interprets the invisible God within us. *(Begotten only of God, [1]monogenes. Official guide, [2]eksegesato, from ek, preposition denoting source, and hegeomai, the strengthened form of ago, to lead as a shepherd leads his sheep; thus hegeomai means to be officially appointed in a position of authority.)*

1:19 The Jews sent a delegation of priests and Levites from Jerusalem to question John the Baptist; this is how he responded to them when asked, "So who are you really?"

1:20 Without hesitation he made it clear to them that he was not to be confused with the Christ.

1:21 "Could you possibly be the re-incarnate Elijah?" To which he answered, "No, I am certainly not!" Then you must be The Prophet Moses said would come? "No!" He said, "I am not." *[Deut 18:15; John 6:14; Acts 3:22]*

1:22 So who are you then? How shall we respond to those who sent us? What would you say about yourself.

1:23 I echo the prophetic voice of Isaiah, crying with urgency in the wilderness, "At once! Level the highway of the Lord! His appearance is apparent, without delay!"

1:24 These priests and Levites sent to question John were all of the Pharisee Party.

1:25 "So if you are not the Messiah, neither Elijah, nor that Prophet, what is the purpose and significance of your baptism then?"

1:26 John replied, "I baptize in water; but you do not even recognize him who is standing in your midst!

1:27 My baptism is preparing the way for this one coming after me; I am not here to distract from him in any way, or to make a name for myself! I do not even qualify to be the slave that unties his sandals!

1:28 This conversation was in Bethania, beyond the Jordan, where John was baptizing.

1:29 The next day John saw Jesus approaching him, and declared: "Behold the Lamb of God; this is the one who would [1]lift the [2]sin of the [3]cosmos like an anchor from the sea floor, for mankind to sail free!" *(This is unheard of! It is not about a vengeful god demanding a sacrifice; this is your Father and Creator providing himself as sacrifice. The ultimate sacrifice for sin would never be something we did, or brought to God to appeal to him; the shocking scandal of the cross, is the fact that mankind is confronted with the extravagant, embarrassing proportions of the love of their Maker; Father Son and Spirit would go to the most ridiculous extreme to finally convince us of their heart towards us! In order to persuade us of our worth, God speaks the most severe scapegoat language: "Behold the Lamb of God, who takes away [**airo** - lifts up] the sin [singular] of the world!" This completely disarms religion! Suddenly there is nothing that we can do to persuade God about our sincere intentions; this is God persuading us of their eternal love dream! The word αἴρω - [1]airo, a primary verb; to lift up; by implication to take up or away; specifically to raise the anchor to sail away. See John 12:32 When I am lifted up from the earth, I will draw all judgment to me! Also John 19:15 - Lift him up! Lift him up! Crucify him!" Note, the word [2]sin is singular **hamartian** - sin is not stuff you do, sin is being out of sync with your true identity and thus, missing out on sonship. The word, [3]kosmos in the NT refers to the entire human family and their social structures.)*

1:30 Jesus is what my ministry and prophetic message are all about. Though younger than I, he ranks above me, since he always was! *(See John 1:15)*

1:31 I am not here to [1]introduce him merely as my cousin from a human point of view; my baptism in water is to publicly declare him to Israel as the Messiah whom their Prophets have proclaimed! (*¹I do not know him; meaning my knowledge of him is not reduced to my opinion according to the flesh - I too only know him by revelation, according to the prophetic word. Even though John grew up within the dramatic context of his own supernatural birth, he didn't claim that his knowledge of himself or his cousin Jesus was anything he merely learnt by human opinion or instruction. See Luke 1:5-80.)*

1:32 Then John made this emphatic statement, "I ¹gazed with wonder and saw the Spirit descending ²out of the heavenlies and resting upon him like a ³dove, ⁴endorsing her ⁵abiding anointing on him, thereby uniting heaven and earth in the incarnate Christ!" *(John uses the word, ¹theaomai, to view attentively, to contemplate, to learn by looking; it suggests a gazing with wonder. See 1 John 4:13,14. The preposition ²ek always denotes source or origin. The word for dove in the Greek, ³peristeran is feminine. The preposition ⁴epi suggests a continuous influence upon; to superimpose, to have charge of; thus to endorse! The word ⁵meno means to continue to be present in a seamless union; to abide. It is not as though the Spirit was absent in Jesus' life until now; this coming upon him was the prophetic moment of the Spirit's endorsing of his ministry; uniting heaven and earth in the incarnate Christ.)*

1:33 I did not merely take into account what I knew about Jesus as my cousin according to the flesh, but he who authorized me to immerse people in water clearly instructed me saying, the one upon whom you see the Spirit descends and abides, he is the one who ¹immerses in Holy Spirit. *(John's baptism announces the incarnation; yet it communicates a mere prophetic picture of what Jesus' spirit baptism will fully interpret of mankind's co-inclusion and joint immersion into his death, resurrection and ascension. In the incarnation we have the prophetic word on exhibit, intercepting human history by assuming human form; thus we see divinity immersed into our humanity and declaring that there would be no stopping him from entering into our hell and deepest darkness. In dying our death, God would bring closure to every destructive mindset and futile fruit we inherited from Adam's fall. Just as he was raised out of the water in his baptism, we would be co-elevated together with him in his resurrection into newness of life! Hosea 6:2; Ephesians 2:5. The word ¹baptizo from bapto, to immerse, to overwhelm.)*

1:34 Having witnessed this exactly as I have told you, I confidently declare that Jesus is indeed the Son of God!

1:35 The following day John was standing with two of his students,

1:36 while gazing intently at Jesus, he announced, "See for yourselves, the Lamb of God!"

1:37 These two students of John listened intently and were obviously intrigued by his words, thus they immediately[1] joined Jesus on his way. *(John uses the word akoloutheō from a, as particle of union plus keleuthos, a road, thus to join someone on the same road, to accompany.)*

1:38 Jesus turned around and looked them in the eyes and asked, "What is it that you are really looking for?" They answered him, Rabbi, which means, my Teacher, where do you [1]abide? *(John uses the word [1]meno more than anyone else in the New Testament. Meno means to continue to be present in a seamless union; to abide. This word points to so much more than a mere geographic location or physical address. It is a word key to John's understanding of the revelation of the incarnation; it locates us in that place where he has restored us to, so that we may be where he is, in the bosom of the Father; also that we may know, that just as he is in the Father, so we too are in him and he in us! John 1:18 and John 14:2,3,10 &20. See also 1 John 5:20 This is what has become distinctly clear to us: the coming of the Son of God is God's mission accomplished! He is the incarnate Christ. The moment all of Scripture pointed to, has arrived! The Son is present! In him God has given us the greatest gift, a mind whereby we may know him who is true; and in the same knowing, to find ourselves there in him who is true! Mankind is fully included and located in him, in his Son Jesus Christ; this means that whatever Jesus is as Son, we are. This is the true God; this is the life of the ages!)*

1:39 He replied, "Come along and [1]see for yourselves." They came, saw where he was [2]lodging, and ended up [2]remaining with him for the day. It was late afternoon when this happened. *(John uses the word ὄψεσθε - [1]opsesthe from oraoo, you will see [perceive] for yourselves. Again the word [2]meno is used. Not long after this Jesus might have been homeless because of his public and controversial cleansing of the temple. See Matthew 8:20, "Foxes have dens and the birds have nests..." also Matthew 12:46, While Jesus was still speaking to the crowds, his mother, brothers and sisters stood outside requesting to talk with him.)*

1:40 Andrew, Simon Peter's brother, was one of the two.

1:41 He immediately fetched his own brother Simon, telling him, "We've found the Messiah" which in Greek means, "the Christ." *(Aramaic was the spoken language and Greek the academic language in which the New Testament was written.)*

1:42 When he introduced him to Jesus, he gazed intently at him and said, you are Simon the son of [1]Jonah; you will be [2]known as Mr [3]Rock. *(The Hebrew word **yona**, יונה means dove. The word [2]**kaleo** means to surname, to identify by name. **Kefas** is the Aramaic for [3]**Petros**, a stone or chip of rock - a chip of the old block! See Matthew 16:13 - 18.*

This conversation beautifully reminds of the Song of Songs in chapter 2:14 "Oh my dove [yona], in the clefts of the rock, in the crevice of the cliff, let me see your face, let me hear your voice, for your voice is sweet, and your face is comely. The crevice of the cliff is the address and home of the rock pigeon! The birds have nests!)

1:43 The next day Jesus intentionally departed from there and went to Galilee. There he met Phillip along the way and asked him to accompany him.

1:44 Phillip was from Bethsaida, the hometown of Andrew and Peter. *(The word **koloutheō** is again used; from **a**, as particle of union and **keleuthos**, a road, thus to join someone on the same road, to accompany.)*

1:45 Phillip immediately went looking for Nathaniel and told him the news! We have found the one Moses wrote about in the Torah and he whom the Prophets announced when they spoke about Jesus, [the Savior] the son of Joseph from Nazareth. *(See Deuteronomy 18:15, "The LORD your God will raise up for you a Prophet like me from among you, from your brethren, him you shall heed. Deut 18:18 I will raise up for them a Prophet like you from among their brethren; and I will put my words in his mouth, and he shall speak to them all that I command him. Genesis 49:10, The scepter shall not depart from Judah, nor the ruler's staff from between his feet, until he comes to whom it belongs; and to him shall be the obedience of the peoples. Isaiah 7:14 Therefore the Lord himself will give you a sign. Behold, a virgin shall conceive and bear a son, and you shall call his name Immanuel. Also Isaiah 53:1-12; Isaiah 9:6,7 For unto us a child is born, unto us a Son is given: and the government shall be upon his shoulder: and his name shall be called Wonderful, Counsellor, The mighty God, The everlasting Father, The Prince of Peace. Of the* *increase of his government and peace there shall be no end, upon the throne of David, and upon his kingdom, to order it, and to establish it with judgment and with justice from henceforth even for ever. The zeal of the LORD of hosts will perform this. Daniel 9:24-27; Jeremiah 23:5-6. See also Joh 5:39,40 You search the Scriptures, because you think that in them you have eternal life; and it is they that bear witness to me; yet you refuse to come to me that you may have life. John 5:46, 47 If you believed Moses, you would believe me, for he wrote of me. But if you do not believe his writings, how will you believe my words?")*

1:46 To which Nathaniel answered, "How does Nazareth fit into the picture of God's promised goodness? Phillip said to him, "Come and see for yourself!" *(The τι αγαθον, 'what good thing?' of Nathaniel refers to Scriptures like Jeremiah 33:14 & 15 Behold, the days come, says the LORD, that I will perform that good thing which I have promised. In those days and at that time I will cause a righteous Branch to spring forth for David; and he shall execute justice and righteousness in the land. Also Micah 5:2 But you, Oh Bethlehem Ephrathah, who are the least among the clans of Judah, from you shall come forth for me one who is to be ruler in Israel, whose origin is from of old, from ancient days. Nathanael's question seems to imply, that not Nazareth, but Bethlehem, was to be the birth-place of the Messiah.)*

1:47 When Jesus saw Nathaniel approach him, he made the following observation, "Now here is a man of Israel, in whom there is no guile!" *(Note the wisdom of Jesus, instead of engaging Nathaniel in a doctrinal debate around the Scriptures, he endorses him!)*

1:48 Nathaniel was surprised! How can you possibly know me if we have never met? Jesus answered him, "Long before Phillip spoke to you, I saw you under the fig tree!"

1:49 Nathaniel exclaimed, "Rabbi, you are the Son of God! You are the king of Israel!"

1:50 Jesus said, "So you believe because I said that I saw you sitting under the fig tree? You haven't seen anything yet! *(By this Jesus does not mean the many miracles he is yet to witness, but rather, that his mission was to introduce us to ourselves again, so that we may know even as we have always been known! We have forgotten what manner of people we are! He knew us before he formed us in our mother's womb! James 1:17, 18, 23-25. Jer 1:5; 1 Cor 13:12.)*

1:51 Truly I say unto you *[singular]*, **because of who I am, you** *[plural - You-manity - all the families in heaven and on earth]* **will surely see this communication between the heavenly sphere and earth thrown wide** [1]**open, and the celestial messengers of God ascending and descending upon the incarnate son of man. Heaven and earth meet in the incarnate one!** *(In him every definition of separation and distance is cancelled! Isaiah 55:10,11 "For as the rain and the snow come down from heaven, and return not there without saturating the earth [all flesh], so shall my word be that goes forth from my mouth; it shall not return to me empty, but it shall accomplish that which I purpose, and prosper in the thing for which I sent it. The prophetic word was destined to become flesh; every nook and cranny of human life is saturated in the incarnation! The word* $\alpha\nu\epsilon\omega\gamma o\tau\alpha$ [1]*aneogota, Perfect Active Participle; the one who has led us upward once and for all; from* **anoigō, ana,** *upward and* **agoo,** *to lead! Jesus reminds Nathaniel of Genesis 28:12-14, "And Jacob dreamt that there was a ladder set up on the earth, and the top of it reached to heaven; and behold, the celestial messengers of God were ascending and descending on it! And Jahweh said to him, I am Elohim of Abraham, your seed shall be like the dust of the earth, and you shall spread abroad to the west and to the east and to the north and to the south; and in you and your Seed have all the families of the earth been blessed!" See Ephesians 3:15 and Ephesians 1:3 Let's celebrate God! He lavished every blessing heaven has upon us in Christ!*

Ephesians 4:8, Scripture confirms that he led us as trophies in his triumphant procession on high; he repossessed his gift [likeness] in human form. [*Quote from Ps 67:19 LXX Septuagint,* [1]$\check{\epsilon}\lambda\alpha\beta\epsilon\varsigma$ $\delta\acute{o}\mu\alpha\tau\alpha$ $\acute{\epsilon}\nu$ $\grave{\alpha}\nu\theta\rho\acute{\omega}\pi\omega$, *elabes domata en* [in] **anthropo** *- You have repossessed gifts in human form. The word* **elabes** *from* **lambano** *means to take what is one's own. The word for the human species, male or female is* **anthropos,** *from* **ana,** *upward, and* **tropos,** *manner of life; character; in like manner. [Masoretic Hebrew text, Ps 68:18,19* לקחת מתנות באדם *lakachat mattanoth ba adam - "You have taken gifts in Adam."* **The gifts which Jesus Christ distributes to us he has received in us, in and by virtue of his incarnation!** *Adam Clarke.] We were born anew in his resurrection. 1 Pet 1:3, Hosea 6:2, and Eph 2:6, We are also elevated in his ascension to be equally welcome in the throne room of the heavenly realm where we are now seated together with him in his authority.]*

Ephesians 4:9 The fact that he ascended confirms his victorious descent into the deepest pits of human despair. [See John 3:13, "No one has ascended into heaven but he who descended from heaven, even the son of man." All mankind originate from above; we are **anouthen,** *from above. See James 1:17, 18]*

Ephesians 4:10 He now occupies the ultimate rank of authority from the lowest regions where he stooped down to rescue us to the highest authority in the heavens, having executed his mission to the full. [Fallen mankind is fully restored to the authority of the authentic life of their design. Psa 139:7 Where shall I go from Your Spirit? Or where shall I flee from Your faces? Plural מפניך *mippaneycha Faces of Elohim. The plurality of persons in the Godhead is intended. Psa 139:8 If I go up to Heaven, You!* שמים שם אתה *Shemayim Shem/Sham Atah. The word* שמים *shemayim, the heavens [which is the plural of the next word],* **Shem,** *meaning, name or renown; the identical adverb* **Sham** *meaning, here, there. In Ancient Hebrew,* ᴍᴧᴌᴌ *breath.*

Then the word, אתה *begins with* **Aleph** *and* **Tav** את *AT which are the first and last letters in the Hebrew Alphabet; the Rabbis interpret as the first matter out of which all things were formed, [see Gen 1:1]. The particle AT [pronounced, et], is untranslatable in English; but, says Rabbi Aben Ezra, "it signifies the substance of the thing!" Then follows the letter* ה *hey, in Ancient Hebrew, it is* ✲*, the man with raised hands pictures a sigh of wonder, "behold," as when looking at a great sight; thus, meaning, "breath" or "sigh," as one does when seeing something wonderful and pointing it out. The* ה *[hey] is also the number 5, which is the number for grace! The union of* **Alpha** *and* **Omega** *[which are the first and last letters in Greek], makes the verb* αω*, I breathe. And in Hebrew the union of the first and last letter in their alphabet,* את *[in modern Hebrew] are written,* **Aleph** *[bull's head] and* **Tav** *[the cross]* ✝𝒴 *in Ancient Hebrew!*

If I make my bed in Hades, your presence already fills it! LXX - πάρειμι *pareimi your immediate presence - I am! In the LXX, which is the Greek Septuagint [250 BC] it is Ps 138:8 [139 in the Hebrew text] See my notes on 1 Thess 2:19.*

"Jesus has united heaven and earth, the life of God and human life in himself. Just as it was planned before the time of the ages." Baxter Kruger.)

2:1 Three days later there was a wedding in Cana, a village in Galilee which Jesus' mother attended.

2:2 Jesus and his followers were also invited.

2:3 When Mary learned that they had run out of wine, she informed Jesus.

2:4 He responded with, "Well Ma'am, that's their problem - or do you want me to steal the show here at somebody else's wedding, when my hour of fulfilling my mission has not yet come? *(Religion has run out of wine – Jesus lived aware of his mission which was to redeem and restore the joyous celebration of the union and Romance of the ages – marrying humanity and divinity! While he is the true joy and wine of the party, he fully understood what it would cost him to drink the cup of mankind's injustice and violence on the cross! See John 12:27 "Now is my soul troubled. And what shall I say? 'Father, save me from this hour'? No, for this purpose I have come to this hour.)*

2:5 Mary proceeded to line up the waiters to assist Jesus, "Do whatever he tells you to!"

2:6 Now there were six empty stone water pots used for the ceremonial cleansing of the Jews. They could hold approximately twenty gallons each.

2:7 Jesus asked the waiters to fill these stone jars with water, to the brim. *(Nothing would be left untouched by the effect of the incarnate Word impacting human life entirely - every nook and cranny - spirit soul and body! See Mirror note in John 1:51; also 1 John 5:18.)*

2:8 And then instructed them to immediately draw from the containers and present it to the governor of the feast; which they did without hesitation.

2:9 The host of the event tasted the water that has now become wine, but had no clue as to its vintage or origin. The servants didn't tell him a word, so he called the bridegroom. *(According to tradition, the bridegroom provides the wine for the wedding - Jesus prophetically fulfills the role of the bridegroom here!)*

2:10 "Why would you keep the best wine for last?" Everybody serves the better wine first, so that by the time the cheaper wine is served, no-one can tell the difference - and here you surprise us all by bringing this excellent wine from your storehouse. Even though we already had much to drink, it is impossible

not to tell its superiority! *(Even minds intoxicated with inferior religious jargon can immediately tell the difference when the Holy Spirit transforms ordinary conversation into the wonderful, blissful wine of revelation and the merry celebration of life!)*

2:11 In this first of the signs which Jesus performed at a wedding in Cana of Galilee, he gave everyone a foretaste of the beauty and intention of his mission. And his disciples believed in him. *(The word [1]doxa often translated glory, from **dokeo**, to form an opinion, a view, an idea or intention - ideas become our eyes -the way we see things. [Baxter Kruger]*

If Jesus could do this to water - imagine how he can transform ordinary routine days into the invigorating adventure of living the life of our design!

His 'FIRST' miraculous sign was a change within a vessel! A jar of stone. External washing has been upgraded to internal transformation of inner thought processes. Completely transformed to the "brim"! And, it wasn't even drinking water, but "the kind used for ceremonial washing!" There is nothing Jesus intended to leave out of this transformation. And, although it wasn't time for Jesus to give his wine that night at Cana. I believe it was no accident that it was the first miracle - Could there have been a more profound picture of his ministry and what his Wine would do in the lives of ordinary vessels? He thus revealed his Glory! E Meaney.

"They have no wine." That's all Mary says to Jesus after noticing the newlyweds' embarrassment. Could she be more indirect? Yet he knows what she wants, and he's not feeling ready. He tells her it's not time to reveal his glory and suffer the consequences. The wine he could make would be free to the guests but cost him plenty. Mary marches right over to the serving table as if he'd said "no problem" instead of "no way." She once said a costly yes; she's not about to take no for an answer from him. Because they have no wine. It's human history she's talking about, life's disappointed guests milling around with empty glasses from time immemorial. She's waited long enough for the mighty to fall, for the poor to dance at the wedding, for the kingdom's elixir to flow. Three Persian potentates once bent their knees to him. Why is he still constructing cabinets in Nazareth? She wants him out of the house. He gives in and produces liquid heaven in preposterous quantities. He squanders it on us, the undeserving who can't distinguish rotgut from Rothschild. He becomes the wastrel we need him to be. - Thank you,

Mary." Prayer; When we are reluctant to act on our callings, Oh God, send Mary to remind us, "They have no wine." Get us out of the house. M Luti.)

2:12 After this he joined his family and followers to go down to Capernaum and remained there for several days.

2:13 Jesus then went up to Jerusalem in time for the Jewish Passover.

2:14 When Jesus went into the temple he was shocked to find scores of traders selling their sacrificial items, cattle, sheep and doves. Even their money brokers were comfortably set up in the sanctuary. *(The business of sin-consciousness has taken over the mindset of religion - until Jesus arrives.)*

2:15 Then with a whip that he plaited of small [1]strands, he drove everyone with their sheep and oxen out of the temple and overturned the tables of the money brokers so that their money went flying all over the place. *(Jesus dramatically reveals that his Father has no delight in our religious sacrificial systems and its sin-conscious currencies. [1]σχοῖνος - schoinos perhaps from skenos, tabernacle or skin - leather thongs - a profound prophetic picture of his own broken skin that would become the whip to drive out sin-consciousness from our minds - the ultimate cleansing of the temple - the sanctuary of God within us! 1 Peter 1:18,19.)*

2:16 He also drove the dove traders out with, "How dare you turn my Father's house into a shopping mall?"

2:17 This incident reminded his disciples of the Scripture, "I am consumed with zeal for my Father's house!" *(Psalm 69:9. God is ablaze with zeal for you! You are the temple of God - his address - his dwelling!)*

2:18 The Jews demanded to know from Jesus how, what he has just done in the temple, could possibly point to the significance of his Messianic mission. "Show us a sign!"

2:19 To which Jesus responded, "The temple will be completely demolished by you and in three days I will raise it up!" *(The word [1]lusate, to undo, demolish, is in the Aorist, Passive, imperative case; the distinction between the Aorist Imperative and the Present Imperative is one of aspect, not necessarily tense. Thus, to get something over and done with!*

30

See Matthew 12:39,40 But he answered them, "An evil and adulterous generation seeks for a sign; but no sign shall be given to it except the sign of the Prophet Jonah. For as Jonah was three days and three nights in the belly of the whale, so will the son of man be three days and three nights in the heart of the earth.

"Ask a sign of the LORD your God; let it be deep as Sheol or high as heaven. But you would not, therefore the Lord himself will give you a sign. Behold, a virgin shall conceive and bear a Son, and shall call his name Immanuel." Isaiah 7:11-14. "For unto us a child is born, to us a Son is given; and the government will be upon his shoulder, and his name will be called Wonderful Counsellor, Mighty God, Everlasting Father, Prince of Peace. Of the increase of his government and of peace there will be no end." Isaiah 9:6,7.

In his resurrection on the third day, God would co-quicken the human race and co-raise us together with him! Hosea 6:2, Ephesians 2:5. Human life will again be the tabernacle of God! "On the third day Esther put on her royal robes and stood in the inner court of the king's palace, opposite the king's hall. The king was sitting on his royal throne inside the palace opposite the entrance to the palace; and when the king saw Queen Esther standing in the court, she found favor in his sight and he held out to Esther the golden scepter that was in his hand. Then Esther approached and touched the top of the scepter." Esther 5:1,2

"And beginning with Moses and all the Prophets, he interpreted to them in all the Scriptures the things concerning himself." Luke 24:27 "They said to each other, did not our hearts ignite within us while he talked to us on the road, while he opened to us the Scriptures?" Luke 24:32 "Then he said to them, these are my words which I spoke to you, while I was still with you, that everything written about me in the law of Moses and the Prophets and the Psalms must be fulfilled. Then he opened their minds to understand the Scriptures, and said to them, Thus it is written, that the Christ should suffer and on the third day rise from the dead" Luke 24:44-46; See also Psalm 22 and Isaiah 53.

Matthew 16:21 From that time Jesus began to show his disciples that he must go to Jerusalem and suffer many things from the elders and chief priests and law professors, and be killed, and on the third day be raised.)

2:20 The Jews responded with, "This temple was under construction for forty six years and you will rebuild it in just three days? Haha!"

2:21 They did not understand that the temple Jesus was pointing to, was the human body. *(In him, the only true address of God was to be redeemed in human life in his resurrection! See Hosea 6:2 "After two days he will revive us, on the third day he will raise us up!" Also Ephesians 2:5 and 1 Peter 1:3; Acts 7:47-50 But it was Solomon who built a house for him. Yet the Most High does not dwell in houses made with hands; as the Prophet says, 'heaven is my throne, and earth my footstool. What house will you build for me, says the Lord, or what is the place of my rest? Did not my hand make all these things?'*

*The word **hieros** speaks of the greater temple building with all its outer courts etc. whereas the word Jesus uses here is **naos**, referring to the inner sanctuary - this is also the word Paul uses in 1 Corinthians 6:19 "Do you not realize that your body by design is the sacred shrine of the Spirit of God!" This is the most sacred place in the universe! There is nowhere in eternity that can match this! See John 1:14 "And the Word became flesh and now resides within us! And 14:20 In that day you will know that I am in my Father and you in me and I in you!")*

2:22 These words of Jesus as well as their significant prophetic connection with Scripture gave such clear context to the disciples when they later, after his resurrection, recalled all these things.

2:23 Now during the Passover feast in Jerusalem, many believed in his Name - surely the signs he did confirmed his mission as the Messiah-Savior of the world? *(Passover, or Pasach, פסח protecting and rescuing. From an Arabic root which means to expand; to save. See intro to Luke chapter 4.)*

2:24 Jesus however did not make much of their apparent support - he wouldn't entrust himself to them since he knew all things. *(He knew how their own faith would fail them in the end. He did not endorse their excitement about the signs they saw as a valid basis to their belief. Signs are not the source of faith - signs follow faith! Jesus' belief in the integrity of our inner being is what saves us from the lies that we believed about ourselves.)*

2:25 He knew that their brief belief was simply based on the surface hype of the moment and not upon that which he was about to redeem in their innermost [1]being. He knew them better than what they knew themselves! He had no need for anyone's theory about the [2]human species to confirm what he

always knew to be true about them. (*Literal translation - "He had no need that any should testify concerning human life - he indeed knew what* [1]*was in the human being."* [1]***eimi***, *I am; our very beingness! Which was exactly why he came, not as an example for us but of us! So that we may know even as we have always been known! Matthew 13:44, 2 Corinthians 4:7. The word for the* [2]*human species, male or female is* **anthropos**, *from* **ana**, *upward, and* **tropos**, *manner of life; character; in like manner. See John 1:51.*)

3:1 Now amongst them there was a man who was a prominent leader among the Jews, a Pharisee named Nicodemus.

3:2 He came to see Jesus under the cover of the night and said to him, "Rabbi, it is [1]clear for all of us to see that you [2]come from God as a Teacher - the signs you perform are proof that God is [6]with you! [3]No one is [4]able to do these signs you do [5]if they are not in [6]union with God. *(The thoughts from the following 6 words are repeated in the answer Jesus gives Nicodemus: [1]oidamen, from eido, to perceive, to see; to discern. [2]eleluthas, from erchomai, to come from; [3]oudeis, no one; [4]dunamis, to be capable; able; to have the power to accomplish. [5]ean me, unless; if not; [6]meta, together with; to be included in; to be in union with.)*

3:3 Jesus answered him emphatically; no one would even be able to recognize anything as coming from God's domain unless they are born from above to begin with! The very fact that it is possible to perceive that I am in union with God, as a human being, reveals mankind's genesis from above! *(Notice from the previous verse how Jesus employs a play of words from the question of Nicodemus. Here Jesus uses the word **anouthen** meaning from above - see James 1:17, every good and perfect gift comes **anouthen** [from above])*

3:4 Nicodemus did not understand this answer at all and said to him, "How can a person be born if they are already grown-up? Surely one cannot re-enter your mother's womb and be born a second time? *(Nicodemus looks at the subject merely from the physical side. His "second time" is not the same as Jesus' "from above." As Godet remarks, "he does not understand the difference between a second beginning and a different beginning.")*

3:5 Jesus answered, you have to get this, unless someone is born out of water *(the womb)* and Spirit, there would be no possible connection with the realm of God!

3:6 Whatever originates out of flesh is flesh; but what is sourced in Spirit is spirit! *(The Message says, when you look at a baby, it's just that: a body you can look at and touch. But the person who takes shape within is formed by something you can't see and touch--the Spirit)*

3:7 Don't be so surprised when I say to you*[manity - plural!]* You couldn't get here in the flesh unless you got here from above! *(See John 1:13 These are the ones who discover their genesis in God beyond their natural conception! This is not about our blood lineage or whether we were a wanted or an unwanted child - this is about our God-begotteness; we are his dream come true! We are not the invention of our parents! [You are the greatest idea God has ever had!])*

3:8 We can observe the effect the wind has and hear its sound whenever it touches objects - yet those objects do not define the wind; it comes and goes of its own accord - if life was not born out of spirit in the first place, it would not be possible to detect spirit influence at all! We are spirit-compatible by design! *(Spirit is our origin! Not our mother's womb! See 2 Corinthians 3:3 The fact that you are a Christ-Epistle shines as bright as day! This is what our ministry is all about. The Spirit of God is the living ink. Every trace of the Spirit's influence on the heart is what gives permanence to this conversation. We are not talking law-language here; this is more dynamic and permanent than letters chiselled in stone. This conversation is embroidered in your inner consciousness. [It is the life of your design that grace echoes within you!])*

3:9 To which Nicodemus responded, "How is this possible? What kind of birth can this be?

3:10 You are the teacher of Israel yet you do not know these things?

3:11 Nicodemus, hear me, [amen, amen,] our conversation stems from what we, mankind, have always borne witness to; we endorse what we have observed; how is it that your religious perspectives keep you so blinded to this? *(See Paul's reference in Romans 1:3 The Son of God has his natural lineage from the seed of David; Rom 1:4 however, his powerful resurrection from the dead by the Holy Spirit, locates and confirms his being and sonship in God. Then he says in verse 18 that we can suppress the truth through our own stubborn unbelief, yet in 1:19 he says that God is not a stranger to anyone; whatever can be known of God is evident in every human life. Rom 1:20 God is on display in creation; the very fabric of visible cosmos appeals to reason. It clearly bears witness to the ever present sustaining power and intelligence of the invisible God, leaving mankind without any valid excuse to ignore him. See also Galatians 1:15 God's eternal love dream separated me from my mother's womb; his grace became my identity. Gal 1:16 This is the heart of the gospel that I proclaim; it began with an unveiling of sonship in me; freeing me to announce the same sonship in the masses of non-Jewish people. I felt no immediate* *urgency to compare notes with those who were familiar with Christ from a mere historic point of view.)*

3:12 If I speak incarnate language to you *[Plural - you Jewish law-based-religious leaders)* **and you are not persuaded about our common origin, how will you be persuaded about heavenly things?** *(Here we are person to person - face to face - the prophetic word incarnate!)*

3:13 No one can fully engage in heaven's perspective, unless one's heavenly origin is realized! The Son of man declares mankind's co-genesis from above!

3:14 *(This is my mission: See the prophetic relevance - this is how the veil will be removed!)* **Remember how Moses lifted up the [1]serpent in the wilderness even so the son of man will be lifted up!** *(John 12:31 Now is the judgment of this world, now shall the ruler of this world be cast out; John 12:32 and I, when I am lifted up from the earth, will draw all judgment unto me." John 12:33 He said this to show by what death he was to die. Revelation 12:9. John 3:13 and 14 are most significant since they point to the very essence of the Mission of Jesus - the co-begotteness of the human race now redeemed in our co-crucifixion and co-resurrection on the third day into newness of life! 1 Peter 1:3. The word serpent in the Greek is [1]ophis. See Extended Notes on **Ophis**, the old Serpent at the end of Revelation chapter 12.)*

3:15 In the same prophetic pattern, I will be lifted up for all to see and be equally persuaded in the echo of the life of the ages now redeemed within them!

3:16 The entire [5]cosmos is the object of God's affection! And he is not about to [1]abandon his creation - the [2]gift of his Son is for mankind to realize their origin in him who mirrors their [3]authentic birth - begotten not of flesh but of the Father! *[See John 1:13]* **In this [4]persuasion the life of the ages [4]echoes within the individual and announces that the days of regret and sense of [1]lost-ness are over!** *(The KJV reads, Whoever [4]believes in him shall not [1]perish but have eternal life. The same word translated in the KJV to perish is translated in Luke 15 to be lost. In order to underline the value of the individual, Jesus tells the famous three parables in Luke 15 of the lost sheep, coin and son; now all found, safe and sound! In everyone he repeats the word [1]lost, **apollumi**, to lose, to emphasize the fact that you cannot be lost unless you belong - to begin with! The word [1]**apollumi**, also suggests a sense of uselessness; that which comes to ruin and amounts to nothing! The word [2]**didomi**, to give, in this* *case to give something to someone that already belongs to them; thus, to return. The fact that they already are his own, born from above, they have their beginning and their being in him is now confirmed in their realizing it! He is the "only begotten," ³**monogenes**; begotten only by the Father and not of the flesh; in him we recognize our true beginning - as in the authentic original mold. See my commentary note to John 1:12. The word ⁴**echo**, to hold, or embrace, as in echo. The word, ⁵**kosmos** in the NT refers to the entire human family.)*

3:17 God has no intention to condemn anyone - he sent his Son, not to be the Judge but the Savior of the world.

3:18 Faith and not flesh defines you! In the persuasion of your authentic sonship there is no ¹separation or rejection! For someone to prefer not to embrace this is to remain under their own judgment sustained by their futile efforts to define themselves through personal performance. In their stubborn unbelief they ¹reject what is revealed and redeemed in the Name of the Son, begotten only of the Father and not the flesh. *(The word ¹**krino**, means to separate; to reject; to judge; to condemn. In naming his Son Jesus, the Father openly announces his resolve, which has always been to rescue and redeem his image and likeness in incarnate sonship. As Paul says in Ephesians 3:15 Every family in heaven and on earth originates in him; his is mankind's family name and he remains the authentic identity of every nation. Also in Titus 2:11 The grace of God shines as bright as day making the salvation of mankind undeniably visible. Galatians 1:16 This is the heart of the gospel that I proclaim; it began with an unveiling of sonship in me, freeing me to announce the same sonship in the masses of non-Jewish people. I felt no immediate urgency to compare notes with those who were familiar with Christ from a mere historic and human point of view. See also Hebrews 1:1-3.)*

3:19 And this is the ¹crisis: the light is here right now, yet people are so addicted to their own darkness that they prefer a life of ²labors, annoyances and hardships! *(The word ¹**krisis**, is often translated judgment. The word for evil, ²**poneros**, translates, full of hardships annoyances and labors.)*

3:20 When someone is engaged in something ¹worthless, they often fear exposure and feel threatened by the light! *(The word, ¹**phaulos** means worthless; also used in James 3:16, all kinds of worthless pursuits.)*

3:21 *(But I have good news for you Nicodemus! You won't ever need to hide in darkness again!)* **He who discovers the ¹poetry of truth, faces the light unashamedly - his lifestyle boldly displays the workmanship of union with God! His works speak for themselves -"Made in heaven - wrought in God!"** *(Like Nicodemus there are many following at a "comfortable" distance, hidden in disguise - they too are invited to turn and face the redeeming light of the love of God!)*

3:22 From there Jesus and his followers went to the region of Judea and spend some ¹bonding-time together - ²immersed in conversation. *(The word ¹diatribo carries the idea of a road well travelled; tarrying together - the text says and there he baptized - yet in chapter 4:2 John comments that Jesus himself did not baptize anyone. The word ²baptitso means to immerse; for what it is worth, I thought to reflect on the bonding and cleansing that takes place in conversation, "You are already made clean by the word which I have spoken to you." Jn 15:3. I'm not disputing the fact that water baptism as a cleansing ritual is the context here; but Jesus' baptism shifts the emphasis from the prophetic water symbol to a baptism into words and spirit thoughts. He knows and communicates that his baptism into mankind's death, as the Lamb of God, is what John's prophetic baptism pointed to in the first place.)*

3:23 John and his disciples were not far from there at the Place of Springs, Aenon near Salim, which made it a popular location for baptism.

3:24 This was shortly before John landed up in jail.

3:25 Some of the disciples of John were disputing with a Jew, who was probably baptized by the disciples of Jesus. They debated about the meaning of these purifying rituals - comparing notes as to which baptism would be the most significant between Jesus and John's. *(See Hebrews 6:2* All the Jewish teachings about ceremonial washings *(baptisms),* the laying on of hands *(in order to identify with the slain animal as sacrifice),* and all teachings pertaining to a sin consciousness, including the final resurrection of the dead in order to face judgment, are no longer relevant. *(All of these types and shadows were concluded and fulfilled in Christ, their living substance. His resurrection bears testimony to the judgment that he faced on mankind's behalf and the freedom from an obstructive consciousness of sin that he* *now proclaims. [Rom 4:25; Acts 17:31; Jn 12:31-33] Jesus said, "and when I am lifted up on the cross, I will draw all judgment unto me!" [Heb 9:28])*

3:26 They anxiously informed John that the one who was with him beyond the Jordan, whose life and mission he endorsed and bore witness to, is now attracting everyone to him - his baptism could put them out of business!

3:27 To which John responded, well, he obviously has heaven's backing, so let's not be jealous; everything we have is a gift!

3:28 You heard me when I said that I am not the Messiah - my mission was to introduce the Christ, not to compete with him! **3:29** The Bridegroom's best man does not compete for attention - he is appointed to support the groom and to greatly rejoice when he hears his voice! This is my joy - this is what I have come for!

3:30 The significance of my prophetic mission was simply to elevate him! *(See 1:15 John the Baptist raised his voice to announce emphatically that Jesus was what his ministry and prophetic message were all about. He declared that Jesus, though younger than him, ranks above him and was "born" before him, since he always was!)*

3:31 We are dealing with two dimensions here, the one coming from above presides over all - while the reasoning from a mere earthly perspective is confined to communicate from an earthly point of view. The conversation realized as originating in heaven has the final say. *(See John 3:13 No one can fully engage in heaven's perspective, unless one's heavenly origin is realized! The Son of man declares mankind's co-genesis from above!)*

3:32 Even though I have seen and heard heavenly things, it seems to me that no one embraces what I have borne witness to! By trying to protect a fading prophetic perspective, you are missing the entire point! The shadow is eclipsed by the substance, not the other way around!

3:33 Whoever lays a hold of this testimony has the evidence of God's truth embossed like the impression of a signet ring resonating in their inner consciousness.

3:34 For the one sent from God communicates God's gift language from the limitless resource of the Spirit.

3:35 The theme of this conversation celebrates the extravagant love the Father has for the Son - and in him every gift of God is revealed - his hand extends God's touch; he is God's embrace of the human race!

3:36 To be persuaded about sonship as unveiled in the Son is to fully participate in the life of the ages! To be unpersuaded about sonship is to remain in blindfold mode to life itself in the here and now and to exchange fellowship with the Author of the life of our design for a fearful image of a vengeful, merciless god - quite the opposite of the loving Father the Son reveals!

4:1 Jesus heard the rumors that were spreading amongst the Pharisees, supposing that he was baptizing more people than John.

4:2 The fact was, he didn't baptize anyone himself, his disciples were.

4:3 He then decided to leave the area and go back to Galilee.

4:4 This meant that he had to travel through Samaria. *(At the time the land of Palestine was divided into three parts: Galilee on the north; Samaria in the middle; and Judea on the south.)*

4:5 En-route they approached Sychar, a Samaritan village bordering the field which Joseph inherited from his father Jacob.

4:6 The well which Jacob dug was still in operation. Since it was already midday and Jesus felt exhausted and thirsty from their day and a half walk, *[40 miles from Aenon]* he decided to wait at the well while his disciples would go into the village to buy food. *(Having left the Place of Springs, Aenon early the previous morning, one can just imagine how Jesus' mind drifted to the fountain theme! The life Jesus lived in a human body was no different to ours; he felt the same weariness, hunger and thirst we would, yet he never forgot what manner of man he was. He lived convinced and conscious of who he was. This was his secret; this was how he overcame every temptation victoriously. See Luke 4:2.)*

4:7 When a local Samaritan woman finally arrived to draw water, Jesus immediately asked her for a drink.

4:8 There was still no sign of the disciples.

4:9 The woman obviously anticipated this request and was ready with her response, "You are a Jew, aren't you? So why would you expect to get anything for free from a Samaritan woman?" Within the politics of the day, Jews looked down upon the Samaritans and had no dealings with them. *(She knew very well how strategically en-route this precious well was and what political leverage it gave her over weary Jewish travellers!)*

4:10 *(Jesus was not at all intimidated or embarrassed by her political stance; he didn't allow his awareness of his weariness and desperate thirst, as well as an obvious opportunity to negotiate for a quick fix-drink, to distract from his Person and mission - instead of associating* *himself with the Jews as a mere Jew and endorsing the Samaritan's 'inferior' political identity, he immediately engaged her with a far superior conversation. He escaped the temptation to see himself or the lady reduced to a lesser identity. He knew who he was and what his mission was all about as the Messiah of mankind - by seeing himself he was able to see her in the same light. What he had to offer was not for sale!)* **He looked her in the eye and said, "If you could see the generosity of God's grace gift, you would perceive who I am!** *(I am so much more than a Jewish man and you are so much more than a Samaritan woman!)* **So here I am asking you for a drink when you should be asking me and I would give you the water of life for free!**

4:11 *(Just like Nicodemus in the previous chapter, she struggles to determine which source Jesus was pointing to!)* **Sir, you have nothing to draw with and the well is deep! How would you reach this living water?**

4:12 Whoever you are, [1]you are certainly not greater than our father Jacob who left us this well and its legacy as our inheritance? He bought this land and dug the well; he drank from it himself and it sustained his family and their livestock for centuries. How can you compete with that? *([1]me su meitzon - The interrogative particle, me indicates that a negative answer is expected: Surely you are not superior... The σὺ, you, first in the sentence, is emphatic, and possibly with a shade of contempt.)*

4:13 Jesus answered her, "This well cannot quench the thirst that I am talking about. Anyone drinking from it will thirst again!" *(In her encounter with Jesus her familiar religious and historic identity is dramatically challenged. Everyone who drinks from the wells of religion and politics will thirst again! The business of religion desperately needs paying and returning customers! They crucified Jesus for this reason; their entire system of keeping people dependent on their hierarchy was challenged and condemned! So many sincere Christian ministries today fall into the same snare.)*

4:14 Whoever drinks from the source of this water that I shall give will never thirst again; because the water that I give becomes an artesian well bursting from within, [1]defining the life of the ages! *(The preposition [1]eis, into, indicating the point reached; conclusion; a defining moment. Unlike a man-made hole, dug in the ground to access seepage water, Jesus speaks of a spring of water, an artesian well! In a later chapter this thought is reinforced* *when Jesus declares, "To drink from me is to be persuaded that I am what the Scriptures are all about [then you will discover that you are what I am all about] and rivers of living water will gush out of your innermost being! John 7:37,38 Now this is economic and most effective ministry! In John 16:7 Jesus says, "It is to your advantage that I go!" This is what Paul knew when he wrote "Not only in my presence, but much more in my absence, discover the full extent of salvation in your own heart!" Philippians 2:12. There is something more beneficial to the individual than Paul's next epistle or even his next visit! It is discovering the fountain within your innermost being! The unveiling of Christ in you exceeds your every expectation! Col 1:27. Also Col 2:5 My physical absence does not distance me from you spiritually.)*

4:15 *(Again she did not understand!)* **Sir, then this is what I want! It will save me the trouble to return here again and again to bail out water for my thirst!**

4:16 Jesus said to her, *(you are missing the point! I am not talking about a thirst that water can quench!)* **Picture yourself back at home, you have discussed this with your husband, and before long you** *(you - singular)* **will be right back here, drawing water again from the same old well!**

4:17 The woman answered, "But I have no husband!" Jesus responded with, "This is an honest answer and confirms my point!"

4:18 Marriage does not define you. You could have failed five times and this time you're not sure about committing yourself to the guy you're living with!

4:19 She was shocked! "Sir! Now I know, you are a Prophet!"

4:20 I'm also religious! Our forefathers worshiped here in this mountain; yet you Jews insist that everyone should worship in Jerusalem! *(Maybe feeling a bit vulnerable about her domestic life she tries to change the subject to again emphasize the religious tension between the Jews and Samaritans.)*

4:21 Jesus said unto her, "Believe me lady, the moment everyone was waiting for has come! From now on worship is no longer about a geographic holy mountain - or a sacred city in Israel experience! *(It is not whether you are a Jew in Jerusalem or a Gentile in Japan! The days of prophetic pictures are over!)*

4:22 You have been worshipping in ignorance all along while the Jews continue to anticipate the Messiah in their devotion, knowing that the promise pointing to the Savior of the world would be emerging from within. *(The Samaritans were a mixed race and only received the five books of Moses while they rejected the Prophets. 2Kings 17:28-34.)*

4:23 The end of an era has arrived - ¹the future is here! Whatever prophetic values were expressed in external devotional forms and rituals are now eclipsed in true spirit worship from within, ²face to face with the Father - acknowledging our genesis in him - this is his delight! The Father's desire is the ²worshipper more than the worship! *(Whatever it was that time pointed to, is now present in me. ¹The hour is coming, and now is; **kai nun estin;** See John 5:25 where the same sentence is repeated. The word often translated worship, ²**proskuneo,** from **pros,** face to face and **kuneo,** which I would like to believe to be a derivation of **koinonia,** joint-participation; rather than **kuon** which means dog. I know, some tried to connect the idea of a dog licking its master's hand, which then became a possibility of kissing. I prefer a divine face to face koinonia encounter to define true worship! Although, I do believe that dogs, often referred to as man's best friend because of the very nature of their devotion to their master, has its Greek root connected - **koinonia** is a friendship word to begin with and in it is therefore possible to see its etymological link. This is the only reference to the noun ²**proskunētēs,** worshipper, in the New Testament. See Extended Commentary at the end of the Mirror.)*

4:24 God is Spirit and not a holy mountain or a sacred city with man-made shrines! Return to your Source - the Father is our true fountainhead! *(You are not defined by your physical birth, your domestic life, your history, your culture or your religion!)*

4:25 The women then said, "I know the Messiah is coming, the one who is called the Christ and when he arrives he will declare everything to us from heaven's perspective!"

4:26 Jesus responded to her, "So here I am, speaking to you! I am the One you were longing for."

4:27 Just then his disciples arrived; they were quite surprised that he was in such deep conversation with a woman, but made no remarks.

4:28 Leaving her water pot behind she hurried back to the city to tell the people what happened at the well. *(No water pot can compete with a fountain bursting from within! Suddenly she* *understood that all people indeed share the same origin. The fountain of living water was not distant from her, beyond her reach, but waiting to awaken within her. Not any of her previous five marriages or even her religious tradition could quench her thirst. Not because she failed to meet 'Mr. Perfect' or the men in her life failed to meet her expectation, but simply because of the fact that nothing external was ever meant to define or complete her life.*

The life of our design is defined in Jesus Christ as in a mirror. Here, there remains no partner, politics or past experience to blame or compete with, only a new life within you to discover, explore, enjoy - and share. Your source will sustain you. "By the waters of reflection, my soul remembers who I am." Ps 23

Truth therapy does not attempt to untangle the complicated emotional hurts and traumas of the past; instead truth reveals the integrity of our original life redeemed in Christ. He is the fountainhead of our genesis. Paul did not say, "Behold the old! He said, "Behold all things are new!" 2 Cor 5:17

The end of an era has arrived! Return to your Source. "He is the Author and conclusion of faith." Heb 12:2.)

4:29 "Come quickly! I met a man who told me everything about my life! [1]Could this possibly be the Messiah?" *(With a woman's intuition she avoided* **ouk** *and uses* [1]**mēti**, *whether, at all, perchance. She does not take sides, but piques their curiosity. - Robertson's Word Pictures.)*

4:30 She arose their interest enough for them to leave the city at once to go meet this man for themselves.

4:31 Meanwhile his disciples were urging him to take some food.

4:32 But he said, "I am feasting on food you cannot see!"

4:33 His disciples were baffled, "Who brought him anything to eat?"

4:34 Jesus told them, "My food is to fulfil the desire of him who commissioned me and to leave no detail undone!"

4:35 Would you say that it will take another four months for the seed to ripen in the ear? This is not the food that I am talking about. The fruit of your own toil will never satisfy permanently. I want to show you the real harvest! From now on, look at people differently; see them through your Father's

eyes, and you will know that they are ripe and ready to discover how perfectly mirrored they are in me! *(Jesus cancelled every definition of delay! We've been waiting for the wrong harvest for centuries - the one we've labored for all our lives. A harvest is ripe when the seed in the ear matches the seed that was sown!)*

4:36 This harvest reveals how both he who sows and he who reaps participate in the same joy of the life of the ages!

4:37 Just as the proverb says, "One sows and another reaps!"

4:38 I commissioned you to reap that which you did not labor for! Others labored and you tapped into the fruit of their toil!

4:39 Intrigued by the woman's testimony many of the Samaritans from that city believed! *(They were the first non-pure Jews who tasted the fruit of God's prophetic purpose revealed in Abraham and Israel's history wherein all the nations of the world would be equally included in the blessing of sonship!)*

4:40 They then approached Jesus and entreated him to remain with them longer, so he stayed over for two days.

4:41 When they heard him speak, many more believed.

4:42 They said to the woman, now we believe not just because of your word but we have heard for ourselves and can clearly see that this man is indeed the Christ, the Savior of the world!

4:43 After the two days with them Jesus left for Galilee.

4:44 Explaining why he was heading north to Galilee, John remembers how Jesus repeated the saying that a Prophet is not honored in his own native land.

4:45 The Galileans welcomed him with open arms; they immediately recognized him for the spectacular things he did in Jerusalem where they too had been for the Passover feast.

4:46 So Jesus again visited Cana where he turned the water into wine and there met a man of the royal family whose son was sick in Capernaum.

4:47 This man heard the rumor that Jesus has returned from Judea and was back in Galilee so he went looking for him. When he found him in Cana he entreated Jesus to urgently come with him to Capernaum to heal his son since he was at the point of death.

4:48 Jesus responded with "If your belief in me is merely based on the signs and miracles you can see, you miss the entire point of my mission!" *(See John 2:23-25 and my note on 2:24...Signs are not the source of faith - signs follow faith! Jesus' belief in the integrity of our inner being is what saves us from the lies that we believed about ourselves.)*

4:49 The nobleman urged him to come with him at once before it was too late!

4:50 Jesus then instructed him to return home on his own and said, "your son will live!" And the man believed the word that Jesus spoke and left. *(Here Jesus demonstrates that he didn't come to be restricted to his own human body and physical presence, but as the Word incarnate, his Word will continue to be as he is for all time and everyone! Jesus knows how a father would want to see his son return from the brink of death!)*

4:51 The man was still on his journey home when his servants met him to tell him the good news that his son lives!

4:52 He immediately asked them about the time that his son was healed and they told him it happened at the seventh hour the previous day!

4:53 The father knew that it was the very hour when Jesus declared his son alive! He and his entire household came to faith that day!

4:54 This Jesus did again as a second sign to mark the significance of his ministry beyond Judea into Galilee.

5:1 After these events there was another feast of the Jews in Jerusalem. Jesus determined to be there. *(Pentecost - 50 days after Easter - from the Greek Πεντηκοστή [Pentēkostē] meaning "fiftieth". Traditionally the Feast of Weeks - Shavuot - שָׁבוּעוֹת [Sabbaths] - which is 7 weeks after the 2nd day of Easter - one day after the Sabbath - [49 days] thus 50 days after the lamb was slain! Celebrating the full harvest of the death, descent into hell and the resurrection of Jesus! It is also called the Feast of the "firstfruits of the wheat harvest." See John 12:23,24. "The single grain of wheat died, and did not abide alone!" The Septuagint writers also used the word to signify the year of Jubilee [Leviticus 25:10], an event which occurs every 50th year - celebrating freedom for every slave! See Luke 4:19*

The Shavuot was also the time when Moses received the law - See my notes at the end of Rev 14 - From Mt Sinai to Mt Zion!)

5:2 At the Sheep-gate in Jerusalem there was a pool called Bethesda; in Aramaic it means home of grace and kindness - it had five porches. *(Beth Chesed* בית חסד *- Home of kindness. See Nehemiah 3:1 - the sheep gate [was built near the tower of Hananel* חננאל *- the favor of God] would lead to the market where sheep would be sold for sacrifices - no wonder Jesus was attracted to go there - fifty days ago he was there whip in hand driving out the traders from the temple! [John 2:15] The pool of water reminds of the baptism theme so relevant in John's gospel. Multitudes are still waiting at the typical "prophetic pools" of mercy and kindness for some unmerited sign of favor to come their way! Sitting in the shade of their ideas of the 5 porches [or five-steps to receive blessings from God- ministries] waiting for another "flutter" or "move" of God! Pentecost is the great celebration of the most magnificent move of God, where everything that Jesus accomplished on the cross and in his resurrection is now endorsed and celebrated in the power of the Holy Spirit. Jesus is not just another "move" of God! He is Elohim on the move; the Father and Holy Spirit in the Son made manifest in human skin! He has come to awaken us out of our slumber! This is what Pentecost is all about! See John 7:37,38. "This he said about the Holy Spirit." [Rivers of living waters gushing out of your innermost being!] The true fulfillment of Pentecost unites all 3 prophetic, annual Jewish feasts into one! Pasach,* פסח*, Pentecost and the feast of Tabernacles.)*

5:3 Many ailing people were lying in the shade of these porches; blind, crippled and withered, waiting for the stirring of the water.

5:4 An angel would go down into the pool occasionally to stir the water; the first person to then enter the pool would be healed of whatever it was they were suffering from.

5:5 There was also a man who had an infirmity for thirty eight years.

5:6 Jesus saw this man and realized that he had been there for a very long time; he asked him, "Would you [1]like to be made well right now?" *(θελεις [1]theleis is the Present Active Indicative of the verb thelo - to resolve, desire - not merely, do you wish for something in the future, but, is this your desire right now!)*

5:7 The man answered him, "Sir, I have no one to help me get into the pool when the water is stirred; by the time I get there someone else has already gotten in before me!"

5:8 Jesus said to him, "[1]Arise! Pick up your bed and walk!" *(Jesus boldly speaks resurrection language! [1]egeirō - to awaken or arise from sleep, from disease or from death.)*

5:9 And at once the man became whole and picked up his bed and began to walk! Now this was on the Sabbath day.

5:10 The Jews were immediately offended and rebuked the man for picking up his bed on a day where no work was allowed according to their law! *(Grace offends the legalistic mindset. See Romans 3:27)*

5:11 He answered them, "The man who healed me told me to pick up my bed and walk!"

5:12 They were very keen to know who this man was.

5:13 But the man didn't know who it was who healed him since Jesus already left unnoticed and there were throngs of people around.

5:14 Then a little later Jesus found him in the synagogue and said, "[1]See! You have become whole! Do not continue in your old [2]distorted mindset; then nothing worse can happen to you!" *(It is so important to [1]see your wholeness and not your distortedness! You reflect what you behold. To see yourself through God's eyes is the only way to escape the distortion of contradiction! The word [1]ide from horao means to see, to discern, to perceive. The word translated sin, is the word [1]hamartia, from ha, negative and meros, portion or form, thus to be without your allotted portion or without form, pointing to a disorientated, distorted identity; the word meros, is the stem of morphe, as in 2 Corinthians 3:18 the word metamorphe, with form, is the*

49

opposite of **hamartia** - *without form. Sin is to live out of context with the blueprint of one's design; to behave out of tune with God's original harmony. Hamartia suggests anything that could possibly distract from the awareness of our likeness. See Deuteronomy 32:18, "You have forgotten the Rock that begot you and have gotten out of step with the God who danced with you!" Hebrew,* חול **khul,** *to dance. Many commentators have used this verse to conclude that God punishes people's sin with sickness! This is not the Father whom Jesus reveals! A few verses later [v 22) Jesus emphatically declares that The Father judges no-one! The religious mind has for so long connected God's judgment with disease and sickness! Jesus introduces us to the God who would rather become our distortions and diseases on the cross and go into our darkness and hell to deliver us from its claim, than to send sickness to us and send us to hell! In John 9:2 the followers of Jesus asks "Rabbi, who sinned: this man or his parents, causing him to be born blind?" And Jesus answered, "You're asking the wrong question. You're looking for someone to blame." [Message] Neither this man nor his parents were guilty! Then Knox translates the next sentence to read, "it was so that God's action might declare itself in him!" This has nothing to do with judgment! See also John 9:34 for the typical opinion of the Pharisees! "You were born in utter sin - now you try to teach us!" Nothing makes a Pharisee more nervous and mad than when their sin- and judgment-paradigm gets taken out of the equation!)*

5:15 The man left and told the Jews that it was Jesus who healed him. *(Don't go testify in the wrong place at the wrong time to the wrong audience! That would be like casting pearls before swine!)*

5:16 Unwittingly, this man's testimony confirmed their suspicion and gave the Jews exactly what they wanted, a trigger to launch their persecution of Jesus! They were furious and immediately began to make plans to murder him! Their interpretation of a "Holy Day" was deeply offended! *(Reminds of many sincere Sabbath - keepers today!)*

5:17 Jesus replied, "My Father is working ¹until ²now, and so am I!" *(This is not what the Jews wanted to hear! But Jesus is speaking about a different Sabbath! Just like John reminds us in chapter 2 that he had a different temple in mind; one that he would rebuild in 3 days! And in the next chapter with Nicodemus he points to a different birth; not his mother's womb, but our joint-genesis from above! Then the Samaritan woman in chapter 4 discovers a different well; one that bursts forth from within! So here in chapter 5 Jesus sees a different Sabbath to Jewish sentiment! The Sabbath of God points to his perfect work of both revealing and redeeming his image and likeness in human* *form. Every Sabbath continues to celebrate the perfection of our Father's work - ¹until ²now! So when Jesus heals people on the Sabbath he is not contradicting it, but endorsing it! Jesus is what the Sabbath is all about! He is the substance of every prophetic shadow! In restoring someone's wholeness, the idea of the original Sabbath is reinforced and not compromised! When God introduced the Sabbath it was always meant to be a prophetic opportunity to celebrate his rest, which was him seeing his perfect work unveiled in us! He continues to invite us to enter into his Rest where we cease from our own works! The announcement, "You shall do NO WORK!" was to remind us again and again that his work is perfect, and we cannot improve on it! You cannot improve on you! You are his workmanship - his masterpiece! The deadly fruit of the "I am not Tree - system" had to be thoroughly uprooted! Hebrews 4:4 [Read the entire chapter 4 in the Mirror] Scripture records the seventh day to be the prophetic celebration of God's perfect work. What God saw satisfied his scrutiny. [Behold, it is very good, and God rested from all his work. Gen 1:31, 2:2. God saw more than his perfect image in Adam, he also saw the Lamb and his perfect work of redemption! "The Lamb having been slain from the foundation of the world." Rev 13:8, "That which has been is now; that which is to be, already has been." Ecc 3:15. Also 2 Tim 1:9.] Hebrews 4:10 God's rest celebrates his finished work; whoever enters into God's rest immediately abandons his own efforts to compliment what God has already perfected. [The language of the law is "do;" the language of grace is "done."]*

Faith is God's language; God calls things which are not [visible yet] as though they were. Rom 4:17.

The word ¹heous is a conjunction linking God's work and intent in synchrony with the word ²arti, which already suggests a continuation of a moment "until now!" [See note on arti in 1 Corinthians 13:12,13])

5:18 This was fuel for the fire of Jewish zeal in their determination to execute Jesus! Not only did he break their Sabbath, but now he has gone beyond all extremes! He calls God his own Father - who does he think he is - God's equal?

5:19 Jesus explained to them with utmost certainty that whatever they see the Son does, mirrors the Father - he does not act independent of his Father - the Son's gaze is fixed in order to accurately interpret and repeat what he sees his Father does! The one reveals the other without compromise or distraction! *(The incarnation does not interrupt what the Word was from the beginning - face to face with God!)*

5:20 For the Father and the Son are [1]best of friends! They have no secrets; the Father gladly lets his Son in on everything he does and will continue to show him works of most significant proportions, which will astound you! *(The Father loves [[1]phileo] the Son with fondness.)*

5:21 For just as the Father awakens people from their death-sleep and revitalizes them with Zoe-life, even so it pleases the Son to awaken people to life!

5:22 For the Father judges no-one but has given all judgment to the Son!

5:23 The Father's desire is that all may value the Son with the same honor wherewith they esteem him - there is no distinction - to dishonor the Son is to dishonor the Father.

5:24 Most certainly do I say unto you that this is the vital transition from dead religion into the very life of the ages - embrace the Son's word with the same persuasion as you would the Father's and you will not know any judgment - the Son gives voice to the Father! *(He is the Father's word made flesh.)*

5:25 Oh how I desire for you to get this! The [1]prophetic hour has come! This is the moment for the dead to hear the voice of the Son of God - C'mon! Hear and live! *(The same sentence is used in John 4:23; the eternal hour, is now! Whatever it was that time pointed to, is now present in me. The verb **erchetai**, is the Present Middle Active tense, which is the timeless present tense, [1]the prophetic, hovering hour, is now; **kai nun estin**)*

5:26 The [1]very self existence within the Father is what he has bestowed upon the Son in order for the Son to [2]radiate the same zoe-life. *(The word [1]hosper from **hos**, in that manner; and **per** , an enclitic particle significant of abundance [thoroughness], that is, emphasis; much, very or ever. The word [2]echo, to have possession of, reminds of the English word echo; thus to resonate, radiate.)*

5:27 The Father has also given the Son of man [1]authentic authority to execute judgment on mankind's behalf! *(The word [1]exousia, often translated authority has two components, **ek**, out of, source and **eimi**, I am!)*

5:28 Do not be alarmed by this, but the hour is coming when those in the [1]graves will hear his voice! *(No-one who ever lived will escape the extent of his righteous judgment! Those who have [1]forgotten who they are will hear his incarnate voice! The word for grave, [1]mnēmeion, memory, suggests a remembrance! Like David prophesies in Psalm 22 when he sees the cross-crisis [krisis - judgment] a thousand years before it happens! His conclusion in verse 27 sums up the triumph of God's resolve! "All the ends of the earth shall [1]remember and turn to the LORD; and all the families of the nations shall worship before him!" See 1 Corinthians 15:21,22 The same mankind who died in a man was raised again in a man. In Adam all died; in Christ all are made alive.)*

5:29 And they will come forth out of their graves - for those who have engaged themselves with that which is beneficial, it will be a resurrection to life - and for those who have done that which is worthless, it will be a resurrection unto [1]judgment. *(In the context of John 6:28 and 29 the work that is required is not a duty to be performed but a gift to be embraced - If our own good behavior could earn us salvation then there would be no point in Jesus dying our death! - This would be in conflict with the essence and crux of the gospel! It reminds of 2 Corinthians 5:10 "For we must all appear before the judgment seat of Christ, so that each one may receive good or evil, according to what he has done in the body!" Now read this verse in the Mirror - 2 Corinthians 5:10 For we have all been [1]thoroughly scrutinized in the [2]judgment of Jesus. We are [3]taken care of and restored to the life of our design, regardless of what happened to us in our individual lives, whatever amazing or meaningless things we encountered in the body. (See 5:14,16. We are mirrored in his life; his life reflects ours, not as an example for us but of us. See 2 Corinthians 3:18. The word, [1]phaneroo, means to render apparent, to openly declare, to manifest. Paul uses the Aorist Passive Infinitive tense phanerothenai, not referring to a future event. The Aorist Infinitive presents the action expressed by the verb as a completed unit with a beginning and end. The word, bematos, comes from [2]bayma, means footprint, also referring to a raised place mounted by steps, or a tribunal, the official seat of a judge The word, [3]komitzo, comes from kolumbos, meaning to tend, to take care of, to provide for, to carry off from harm. Paul's reference was not about how much abuse and affliction he suffered, neither was it the many good times he remembered that defined him; "I am what I am by the grace of God!" If we are still to be judged for good or bad deeds that we performed in the body, then the judgment that Jesus faced on mankind's behalf was irrelevant. Galatians 2:21 I do not set aside the grace of God, for if righteousness could be gained through the law, Christ died for nothing! NIV [See also 2 Cor 5:14,16. We are mirrored in his life; his life reflects* *ours, not as an example for us but of us. As well as* 2 *Corinthians 3:18 The days of window-shopping are over! Now, with unveiled faces we are gazing at the glory of the Lord as in a mirror and metaporhe happens - image and likeness awakens within us!] See my* **Extended Commentary Notes** *after the final chapter of the Mirror- Thoughts on Judgment and Resurrection.)*

5:30 The dynamic of my doing is in my union with my Father; my intimate acquaintance with his voice is what inspires me - as I hear, I discern and my judgment is just; there is no conflicting interest here - my Father's commission is my mission in life! *(Proverbs 20:12 The hearing ear and the seeing eye, the LORD has made them both. See Hebrews 5:8 Acquainted with sonship he was* in the habit of hearing from above; what he heard distanced him from the effect of what he had suffered. *(The word often translated as obedience is the word,* **upoakuo,** *under the influence of hearing, or hearing from above. "By" the things he suffered,* **apo,** *away from, distanced. "Then I said, I read in your book what you wrote about me; so here I am, I have come to fulfill your will." [Heb 10:7]) Heb 5:9 By* his perfect hearing he forever freed mankind to hear what he had heard. *[He now makes it possible for us to hear in such a way that we may participate again in the full release of our original identity; the logos finding voice in the incarnation in us.])*

5:31 If this was just about me trying to make a name for myself then you can certainly reject my testimony as phony!

5:32 Yet there is someone else who endorses who I am and I recognize his testimony of me as absolutely true.

5:33 You cross examined John and he too gave testimony to the truth of who I am.

5:34 I do not draw my inspiration from your applause; I'm not here to win a few votes for a noble cause - I am on a rescue mission!

5:35 John was a man on fire, a bright beaming light and for a brief moment you were jumping with joy in his radiance.

5:36 My testimony exceeds John's since the work which my Father has ordained me to finish gives ultimate context to my mission.

5:37 The Father himself who has sent me continues to bear witness to me; yet you are not familiar with his voice and did not discern his prophetic utterance throughout ancient times and therefore you could not recognize his image nor do you realize his appearance at this present time *[in the incarnate word.]*

5:38 Your doubting him whom the Father has sent shows that you have not taken his word to its full conclusion.

5:39 You scrutinize the Scriptures tirelessly, assuming that in them you ¹embrace the life of the ages - yet I am what the Scriptures are all about! *(¹Echo, to hold, embrace, resonate)*

5:40 Still you refuse to resort to me as the very source of the life you seek. *(I echo the life of the ages within you!)*

5:41 I am not anchoring my belief in people's opinion.

5:42 But what I observe about you, is that God's love does not resonate within you! *(You're so obsessed with the rule book that all you see in it is a god of judgment and wrath and miss out on God's love!)*

5:43 Here I am representing my Father and you have a problem with that; yet someone completely unknown to anyone would come in his own name and you will give him your full support. *(How strikingly has this been verified in the history of the Jews! From the time of Jesus Christ to our time, sixty-four false Christs have been reckoned by whom they have been deceived. [Bengel 1750].)*

5:44 How is it possible for you to even venture into the dimensions of faith, if you already have your minds made up to go with popular opinion within your own ranks, while you show no desire to esteem him who proceeds directly from God?

5:45 No, I am not the one to accuse you before the Father - you stand condemned before your trusted friend Moses!

5:46 Had you discerned my Father's voice in Moses you would have been persuaded about me in his writings. *(The significance of the Scriptures is not in themselves but in who they point to! Genesis 3:15; Genesis 12:3 "in you shall all the families of the earth be blessed!" Compare John 8:56 & 58; Genesis 49:10; also Deuteronomy 18:15. "For he wrote of me" - peri gar emou ekeinos egrapsen. Deuteronomy 18:18 is quoted by Peter in Acts 3:22 as a prophecy of Christ and also by Stephen in Acts 7:37. See also John 3:14 about the brazen serpent and John 8:56 about Abraham foreseeing Christ's day. Moses most certainly wrote concerning him.)*

5:47 If you already doubt his words to begin with, my conversation will be irrelevant to you.

6:1 In the course of [1]time Jesus went from Jerusalem across the sea of Galilee which was also called Tiberias. *(With this... meta tauta, is John's favorite general note of the order of events; not necessarily in chronological order. [1]In the context and sequence of time, this would be the following year after the events described in the 1st 5 chapters.)*

6:2 By now a great multitude was following him because of the spectacular healings he performed.

6:3 Jesus went into the hills to be alone with his disciples.

6:4 This was again near the annual Passover. *(Here John reminds us of the economy of Jesus' ministry he knew very well the pivotal significance of his appointment with the ultimate Passover where he would lay down his life as the Lamb of God to be slaughtered by his own creation for their salvation.)*

6:5 There was no getting away from the crowds though; when Jesus saw the multitude arrive he said to Phillip, "How do you think we are going to feed all these people?"

6:6 This wasn't a trick question, but simply to engage their faith; he already knew exactly what he was going to do! *(Jesus was not about to be distracted by the enormity of his mission where his body would be broken at the highest price in order to feed the multitudes of mankind with the true bread from heaven! Just like in Chapter 24 of Luke - the picture of a meal always translates into incarnation language - bread becomes flesh!)*

6:7 Phillip immediately concluded that this was impossible to do and far beyond a budget of any reasonable calculation; two hundred days wages could never buy enough for each person in the crowd to even get a little morsel of bread! *(Mankind cannot redeem themselves! Again, Jesus leads the conversation into a different dimension - like with Nicodemus and the Samaritan woman - he points to a different source; not related to external reasoning or challenges to be met with personal contributions of our own toil or labor to define or defend ourselves but simply accessing the Father's limitless resources within. He has come to free our minds from the restrictions of a dimension that could never truly define us! He dramatically and very intentionally disengages us with every effort of our own to save ourselves! Our salvation is beyond our budget! BUT WAIT!! What about the little lad!? For unto us a child is born, remember!)*

6:8 Then one of his disciples, Andrew, the brother of Simon Peter

6:9 pointed to a little boy who had five small loaves of inexpensive barley bread and two small fishes and remarked how insignificant they appeared amongst such a multitude of hungry people!

6:10 Jesus asked his disciples to get everybody seated - the place was ideal for a picnic since it was spring and the grass was lush and green! Thousands of people gathered! *(In the Jewish custom where only the men were counted there happened to be 5000 of them let alone the multitudes of ladies and children!)*

6:11 Jesus took the bread and fish and thanked God for it, then distributed it amongst the people; everyone was free to take as much as they wanted!

6:12 When the crowd had eaten their fill Jesus said to his disciples to gather up all the broken pieces to make sure that nothing is lost. *(Every fragment and detail of God's masterful work of redeeming mankind in Christ is most significant!)*

6:13 So they did and filled twelve baskets with fragments after everybody had as much as they could eat!

6:14 The people who witnessed these signs [1]began to be more and more convinced that Jesus must truly be that Prophet, the one whom their Scriptures pointed to. *(Deuteronomy 18:15 "The LORD your God will raise up for you a Prophet like me from among you, from your brethren--him you shall heed-- The word [1]elegon is an inchoative imperfect form of the verb; thus, they began to say; the inchoative verb, sometimes called an inceptive verb, shows a process of beginning or becoming.)*

6:15 They were now ready to forcefully grab him and crown him as their King, but when Jesus saw their enthusiasm he slipped away and went higher into the mountain to be by himself.

6:16 In the evening his disciples went down to the sea;

6:17 they were hoping that Jesus would join them and waited until dark but then finally embarked the ship and proceeded to sail across to Capernaum.

6:18 En-route a massive storm hit them with huge swells and strong winds.

6:19 They were now about halfway across the six mile stretch of water, struggling with their oars against the wind and raging waters when they suddenly noticed Jesus coming towards them, walking on the stormy seas! They were horrified!

6:20 He spoke to them and said, "Here I am - you have no reason to fear!" (*ἐγώ εἰμι· μὴ φοβεῖσθε* - *His I am-ness is closer to you than any sense you could ever have of his absence!*)

6:21 They were very happy to take him on board and then miraculously reached their destination in no time!

6:22 The crowd that was left behind saw that there was only one boat and also noticed that Jesus did not leave with his disciples.

6:23 The next day other boats from Tiberias arrived near the area where they ate that bread which the Lord blessed.

6:24 When they realized that neither Jesus nor any of his disciples were around, they got into the boats to go to Capernaum hoping to find Jesus there.

6:25 They found him on the other side and wanted to know how he got there?

6:26 Jesus responded with, Surely the reason why you are so drawn to me is not because of the signs you've seen, but the contentment you felt within you when you ate the bread. (*The destiny of Jesus was not to merely engage people with the miraculous signs - as much as he desired to communicate the essence of his mission - which was to celebrate the incarnation! The bold exhibit of the image and likeness of our invisible Father in us, in human form! Every meal is a celebration of the incarnation. In Luke's interview with the two followers on their way back to Emmaus, he finally records the climax of their encounter with the "Stranger" when he broke the bread and their eyes were opened and they recognized him! The revelation of the incarnation is the point, not another ten miracles!*)

6:27 Living from meal to meal can keep you busy - there is so much more to life than survival - toiling merely for that which perishes is such a waste! The life of the ages requires a different kind of labor! This labor is not the kind which rewards you for something you have done but blesses you with the gift of humanity's Son - this gift of sonship celebrates the authentic life which God the Father has endorsed from the beginning.

6:28 They immediately wanted the recipe! Tell us then what we must do in order to accomplish God's work?

6:29 This is the work of God; your belief in the One whom he has sent! *(Even your ability to believe is God's work! Realizing your authentic sonship on exhibit in Jesus is God's gift to you and cannot be earned! How can your labor compete with what God's rest celebrates as complete!)*

6:30 So Jesus, if it is your job to get us to believe, we need to see more signs!

6:31 How do you compete with Moses? Our fathers ate the manna in the wilderness - as it is written - He gave them bread from heaven to eat. *(The rabbis quoted Psalm 72:16 to prove that the Messiah, when he comes, will outdo Moses with manna from heaven. Robertson's Word Pictures.*

Ps 72:16 "There shall be a handful of corn in the earth upon the top of the mountains; the fruit thereof shall shake like the cedars of Lebanon: and they of the city shall flourish like grass of the earth. KJV [A handful of corn - five loaves here and in the following year's Passover Jesus' own body would be the bread broken on the mount of Golgotha!]

Deuteronomy 8:3 And he [1]treated you gently in the wilderness of your unbelief and fed your hunger there with manna, which you did not know, nor did your fathers know; that he might show you that there is a bread that comes from above, that you did not labor for! Your labor and achievement can never satisfy your deepest longings. The life of our design hungers to be completely sustained by [2]that Word which proceeds out of the mouth of the LORD. [Some translations say, "[1]humbled you" but in 2 Samuel 22:36 the word [1]ענוה Anahvah is translated, "Your [1]gentleness made me great." We are designed to live by [2]every Word which proceeds out of the mouth of the LORD. The Hebrew word כל Kohl from כלל Kalal, often translated, "every" actually means complete; thus, the word in its most complete context. The destiny of the word was so much more than a scroll or page in a book, it always was the Incarnation - Jesus, the Word made flesh!]

He freed us from our slavery and led us gently like a shepherd through the wilderness of our own unbelief and made known to us that our authentic hunger is not for the bread we labor for, but, just like the prophetic picture of manna from above, we can only be truly satisfied by the Word from above; that Word which mirrors our redeemed joint-genesis and eternal oneness!)

6:32 Jesus reminded them that it wasn't Moses who gave them the bread from heaven - My Father is the one who gives the real bread from heaven! *(The manna was a prophetic pointer to the Messiah!)*

6:33 For the bread from God that comes down from heaven is that which gives life to the entire world! *(Mankind is designed, not to define life by the bread-harvest of their own labor, but by daily feasting on **every** **Word** that proceeds from God's mouth, mirrored in its most complete language, the Incarnation. The Hebrew word translated, **every**, is the word, בל **Kohl** from בלל **Kalal** which means complete - thus, the word in its most complete context, which is the Incarnation, the Word that is face to face before God from before time was, is now made flesh, radiating the invisible Father's character and image in human form, as in a mirror! The incarnation is the global language of the Planet! Paul says in 2 Cor 3:2,3, The living Epistle is known and read by all in their mother-tongue language.)*

6:34 They said, Oh Lord, this is the bread we crave! Give us this bread!

6:35 Jesus said, I am the bread of life! He that comes face to face with me shall never hunger and he who finds his faith resting in me shall never thirst!

6:36 But even though you have seen me, you are not persuaded. *(You might be happy with the healings and be entertained by the signs, but still you fail to understand who I am! I'm not here to impress you with me! I'm here to persuade you about you! Your sonship is what I am all about! And the only way that I can persuade you about you is to take you with me into your death and darkness and overcome your fear and hell and birth you again into newness of life in my resurrection!)*

6:37 Everyone whom the Father has given me will come [1]face to face with me! And here, mirrored in me they will see that I am not the Judge! I will not cast anyone out! *(The preposition **pros**, is used here again as in John 1:1.)*

6:38 For I have stepped down out of heaven, not to make a name for myself! I did not come to become a mere historic

hero! I have come to communicate the resolve of him who sent me! *(I am here to demonstrate to you how persuaded my Father is about you!)*

6:39 My Sender's desire is for me to rescue every single individual - [1]this is his gift to me - that I will lose [2]no detail of their original identity mirrored in me! My rescuing mission will conclude in their joint-resurrection! This is the [3]completeness of time! *(This is his gift to me, [1]ho dedoke moi. The phrase, [2]hina pan apoleso ex auto, meaning, that I should lose nothing out of it. In the conclusion/fullness of time - [3]te eschate hemera - This phrase occurs only in John - John 6:39, 6:40, 6:44, 6:54. See John 4:23 The end of an era has arrived - the future is here! Whatever prophetic values were expressed in external devotional forms and rituals are now eclipsed in true spirit worship from within - face to face with the Father - acknowledging our genesis in him - this is his delight! The Father's desire is the worshipper more than the worship!)*

6:40 And this is the desire of my Father, that everyone who [1]sees the Son, through his eyes, and finds the conclusion of *(eis)* their persuasion in him, will resonate *(echo)* the life of the ages! And I will [2]raise him up in the [3]final day! *(Jesus speaks here of mankind's joint resurrection in his resurrection as the final day! The word [1]theōreo means to gaze attentively. See Hosea 6:2 After two days he will revive us; [2]on the third day he will raise us up, that we may live before him. The word [3]eschatos means extreme; last in time or in space; the uttermost part, the final conclusion. What God said about 'you-manity' in their co-resurrection in Jesus, defines eschatology! Heb 1:1-3; Eph 2:5,6. See Rev 20:5 on the First Resurrection.)*

6:41 The religious Jews were no longer paying any attention - they were shocked and offended at the idea that he said he was the bread from heaven!

6:42 They reasoned that since they knew his parents to be Joseph and Mary, he had no valid claim to any heavenly Source!

6:43 Then Jesus addressed them saying, Your murmuring and reasoning amongst yourselves will continue to veil me from you. *(Knowing me from a human point of view will not satisfy your quest.)*

6:44 No one is forcing you to believe - it is the Father who sent me who draws you to see me [1]face to face - only once you've seen how in the mystery of God I mirror you, will you understand that I will co-raise you in the grand-finale of my mission! *(The word [1]pros is used again, face to face.)*

6:45 It is written in the Prophets that every single individual will be taught of God. To hear the Father's instruction concerning me, is to come [1]face to face with me. *(The word [1]pros is used again. See Isaiah 54:13; Jeremiah 31:34 And no longer shall each man teach his neighbor and each his brother, saying, 'Know the LORD,' for they shall all know me, from the least of them to the greatest, says the LORD; for I will forgive their iniquity, and I will remember their sin no more."; Mica 4:1-4)*

6:46 No one has [2]seen the Father except the one who [1]proceeds from him; he is most intimately [2]acquainted with the Father! *(The word [1]para, a preposition indicating close proximity, a thing proceeding from a sphere of influence, with a suggestion of union of place of residence; intimate connection; the word [2]horaō means to gaze; to see with the mind; to perceive; know; to become acquainted with by experience.)*

6:47 Of [1]absolute certainty do I declare to you that anyone whose faith [2]ultimately rests in who I really am, in this one the life of the ages resonates. *(In repeating the words, [1]amen amen - Jesus speaks mirror language in order to emphasize the radiance and resonance of certainty between himself and his audience - from faith to faith. The preposition [2]eis suggests a point reached in conclusion.)*

6:48 I am the bread of life!

6:49 Your fathers ate the manna in the wilderness and died there in the wilderness. *(The manna didn't kill them, their unbelief in themselves did. See Numbers 13:33 and Hebrews 4:2-6. The manna was a mere prophetic shadow of me.)*

6:50 This, what you have here in me standing face to face with you, is the very sustenance of your life; the bread descending out of the heavenly sphere for everyone to eat their fill and not die.

6:51 I am the living bread, I stepped out of the heavenly realm into this earth suit, in the incarnation, so that everyone may feast on the idea of their true incarnate identity mirrored in me and discover the life of the ages incarnate in them! The bread that I will give is my own flesh; it will translate into life for the entire cosmos! *(The word, kosmos in the NT refers to the entire human family.)*

6:52 This brought about a war of words among the Jews! How can this man give us human flesh to eat? *(Just like Nicodemus and the Samaritan woman at the well they again got it all wrong! Jesus was pointing to a different womb, well and meal!)*

6:53 *(Instead of softening the blow by explaining to them what he really meant, Jesus made it a hundred times worse for their religious reasoning, by saying the following!)* **Amen amen, I say unto you that you have** *(echo)* **no real life in yourselves until you consume the flesh of the Son of man and drink his blood.** *(The very core of our beingness is founded in our co-association with Jesus, the son of man; it is only in realizing and fully assimilating our oneness in flesh-incarnate context as the son of man, that we discover the truth of our oneness in our joint-genesis as sons of Deity. He is about to take mankind with him into their death, grave and hell and then victoriously co-quicken them and co-raise them into newness of life!)*

6:54 Your [1]every meal is a celebration of the incarnation; to eat my flesh and drink my blood is to digest me like your body is designed to digest food and it becomes flesh; this echoes the life of the ages and communicates the fact that you are co-risen with me in the final conclusion of my work of redemption. *(The words [1]ho trōgōn, are the Present Active Participle form of the verb to emphasize a continual or habitual eating.)*

6:55 My flesh is food in its truest form and my blood is drink in its truest form.

6:56 The eating of my flesh and drinking of my blood is the celebration of our seamless union - you in me and I in you - because you won't find you until you find me! *(Thoughts eat words like your mouth eats food - both become flesh!)*

6:57 As the living Father has sent me and also sustains me so will I sustain the one eating me. I live through my Father - just like my daily food sustains me, so his life permanently resides in me - now you may also continually and habitually feast on me and live through me!

6:58 This is the bread that stepped down out of the heavenly sphere - there is no comparison with the manna your fathers received from heaven *[which was merely a prophetic shadow pointing to me]*; **they ate and they died** *[without completing* *their destiny]* - **now feast on me and celebrate the life of the ages.** *(Eating and drinking is most significant - every meal is both a reminder and celebration of the incarnation! Every time we face food we are reminded of our beingness in flesh and our seamless oneness with our Maker and one another. See 1 Corinthians 11:26 Your every meal makes the mandate of his coming [1]relevant and communicates the meaning of the new covenant. [Whether you eat or drink, you are declaring your joint inclusion in his death and resurrection, confirming your redeemed innocence. Some translations read, "until I come..." The word translated until is, [1]**achri**, from **akmen**, which means extremity, conclusion, the present time; Jesus is the conclusion of prophetic time! The word **erchomai**, to come is in the Aorist tense, **elthe** - pointing to that which has already happened!]*

The prophetic picture of the table was very strategic in the tent tabernacle in the wilderness - the priests had to daily place fresh bread on the table in the sanctuary. It was called Showbread, לחם הפנים *lechem haPānīm, literally: Face-bread or Bread of the Presence. The Hebrew word for presence means face to face! While Jesus spoke to the two on their way to Emmaus in Luk 24, they did not recognize him, even though their hearts ignited while he was explaining the prophetic promise of mankind's redemption in all of Scripture, from Moses through the Psalms and the Prophets. In Luke's interview, he pressed them for the detail, he wanted to know exactly at what point in their meeting with Jesus did they recognize him in person! He writes in verse 28, "So they drew near to the village to which they were going. He appeared to be going further..." Wow! Should Jesus not at this point have given them an opportunity to make a commitment or at least say a "sinners prayer"? Not even the best Rabbi could take them any further, Luk 24:29 But they constrained him, saying, "Stay with us, for it is toward evening and the day is now far spent." So he went in to stay with them. Luk 24:30 When he was at table with them, he took the bread and blessed, and broke it, and gave it to them.*

Luk 24:31 And their eyes were opened and they recognized him; and he vanished out of their sight.

He vanished from their sight because Jesus can no longer be any more present in his person than what he is present in the Word incarnate in us!

The moment we discover Jesus in Scripture as in a mirror, our hearts ignite and our very next meal becomes a celebration of our incarnate union! "Every time you eat or drink, remember me!" Every meal celebrates the temple! Your body is God's address on planet earth! He does not dwell in buildings made by human hands. You will never again need to employ your willpower to diet and get into shape! Willpower is the language of the law! Love and value-consciousness ignites belief. The revelation of the truth sets you free to be free indeed! The days of fast food and junk-food are over! The Table is sacred and celebrates your body as the sanctuary of your redeemed life, the life of your authentic design! Sitting around the table is a feast of friendship and delightful conversation. Eat food that blesses the temple! Most diseases are diet-related! Study nutrition! We have this treasure in earthen vessels! The vessel takes its value from the treasure it holds! Feast your mind on likeness realities - make Deity your diet - digest me! Face your Father!)

6:59 Jesus said these things in a synagogue while teaching in Capernaum.

6:60 Many of his followers said, this teaching is to tough to chew on!

6:61 Jesus perceived what they were murmuring about and said, So you take offence at this?

6:62 What if you see the son of [1]man *[representing the human race]* **ascending to where he [2]was before?** *(The word for the [1]human species, male or female is **anthropos**, from **ana**, upward, and **tropos**, manner of life; character; in like manner. See John 1:51. Also John 3:13: No one can fully engage in heaven's perspective, unless one's heavenly origin is realized! The Son of man declares mankind's co-genesis from above! John 1:1 In the beginning [2]was the Word [[2]I am] and the word [2]was [[2]I am] face to face with God.)*

6:63 It is the Spirit that quickens the poetry of life - the flesh *(muscle and willpower)* **is useless without the spirit. The words that I speak unto you they are spirit and life! I communicate from a different dimension and perspective giving voice and substance to every prophetic shadow and purpose.**

6:64 I notice that there are those among you who are not persuaded about me. It was clear from the start that even amongst Jesus' close followers there were signs of unbelief and treason. *(And who it was that should betray him - **kai tis estin ho paradōsōn**. Same use of **estin** and note article and Future Active*

*Participle of **paradidōmi**, to hand over, to betray. John does not say here that Jesus knew that Judas would betray him when he chose him as one of the twelve, least of all that he chose him for that purpose. What he does say is that Jesus was not taken by surprise and soon saw signs of treason in Judas. The same verb is used of John's arrest in Matt 4:12. Judas was given his opportunity. He did not have to betray Jesus. Robertson's Word Pictures)*

6:65 I was addressing your hesitance to believe in me when I said to you that no one is forcing you to see yourself [1]mirrored in me - you do not need to go into make-believe-mode or fake your faith - it is the Father's gift to you! *(When you hear the words that I communicate with your heart you will encounter life-quickening faith. To try and decipher my words with your religious reasoning in your head is to miss the entire point of my mission and message. The preposition [1]**pros** - face to face, is translated here as mirrored in me.)*

6:66 Because of this conversation many of his followers went back to their old ways and would no longer be associated with Jesus.

6:67 So Jesus said to the twelve, "Don't feel obliged to stay - you are also free to go if you wish!"

6:68 Simon Peter said, Lord, who is there to go back to - which mirror should we gaze into? Your words resonate the life of the ages!

6:69 We believe and know without a doubt that you are the Messiah, the Christ, the Son of the living God!

6:70 I have [1]pointed all twelve of you to your source and yet one of you remains trapped in the fallen mindset! *(The word **eklego** has traditionally been translated to mean election - I would prefer to emphasize the fact that **ek** is a preposition always pointing to origin or source and the verb **lego**, is associated with its noun **logos** as in the context of John 1:1 The original conversation! See Hebrews 1:1-3)*

6:71 He spoke of Judas, the man of Kerioth, the son of Simon. *(Iscariot was not his surname, but literary means the man of Kerioth, a small town a few miles south of Hebron. Judas was not Galilean like the rest of the disciples, but a Judean and seemed to have struggled more than any of them to see the significance of the mirror likeness of Jesus as defining his true sonship. See reference to Kerioth in Amos 2:2 and then, in Amos 2:5, "because they sell the righteous for silver!" Also the next verse here in John 7:1; then, John 17:12.)*

66

Here is a portion of a most beautiful poem, written by my friend Dusty Harrison - see the entire poem here: https://www.facebook.com/556536215/posts/10155865183711216/

After his suicide was accomplished, Judas lifted up his eyes in a black flame of darkness.
He remembered his betrayal and his defection... his silver thrown... the eyes of his master as he kissed him in the garden.
His thoughts turned in his pain to the words of his master as he spoke them...
Parables of lost things and sorrow filled him...
The lost sheep... wandering off and leaving his flock... and the goodness of the Shepherd leaving the ninety-nine and going after the one... returning with it laid on his shoulders rejoicing...
The woman's lost coin as she searched diligently, sweeping frantically and finally finding it.. and rejoicing and throwing a party for her friends because what had been lost was found and had never lost its value...
The lost Son... and his good Father.
The boy wasting his inheritance...
feeding pigs and longing to return home...
Lost son... the son of perdition.
I have lost none but the son of perdition, he remembered... that the scriptures may be fulfilled... and then...
The skies above both hell and paradise were split... as light poured in... the light that dwarfed even that of paradise... a shout of triumph rained down to him...
and in paradise, a man appeared... a lamb as it had been slain stood with a thief who was jumping and shouting for joy...
The black flame turned to red and yellow...
and the great gulf between paradise was filled with blood like water and across the gulf came the lamb walking on the blood like water... as he approached, the darkness receded and he saw that The Father and Spirit were standing behind him... then his master came close and kissed him on the cheek...
and Judas wept...

7:1 Jesus concentrated most of his ministry activity in Galilee since the Jewish leaders in Judea wanted to kill him.

7:2 This was now about six months later when the Jewish Feast of Tabernacles was at hand.

7:3 His own brothers prompted him to go to Judea so that his followers there might again have the opportunity to witness his signs and teaching, they reasoned.

7:4 They figured that someone of his public importance and stature should not operate in secret! He should show himself off to the world and make a name for himself!

7:5 Yet none of his immediate family believed that he really was the Christ. *(It was only after his resurrection when Jesus also appeared to James that his brother's eyes were opened, 1 Corinthians 15:7 Galatians 1:19. This prompted James to write about seeing the face of your birth when you hear the authentic word of our co-begotteness by the Father of lights. James 1:17,23.)*

7:6 Jesus replied, "My [1]agenda is different from yours! You go ahead and feast with your Jewish friends! *([1]kairos, a fixed and definite time, the decisive epoch waited for.)*

7:7 It is me they hate not you! My testimony exposes their religious rituals and works of self-righteousness as [1]incompetent. *(The word often translated evil, [1]poneros suggests, to be full of labors annoyances and hardships! This word is associated with the system of works righteousness versus faith righteousness.)*

7:8 You go to this feast - I will go when its my time!"

7:9 So his family went to Jerusalem and left him behind in Galilee.

7:10 Then after they were gone he went there unnoticed and kept a low profile.

7:11 The Jews were looking out for him; constantly enquiring about his whereabouts.

7:12 Jesus was the topic of conversation among the people - everyone had an opinion about him. Some said that he was a good man - others thought him to be deceiving the crowds with trickery.

7:13 This was all hush-hush since no-one was prepared to openly oppose Jewish-sentiment.

7:14 Then Jesus surprised them all by showing up midway through the eight-day feast, teaching openly in their temple.

7:15 What amazed the Jews most was his knowledge of Scripture while he never attended any of their schools.

7:16 To which Jesus replied, "My teaching is not the product of my own invention or human perception but by my Divine connection - my mission explains my Sender's purpose.

7:17 Anyone who has a desire to engage with God's heart dream will know without a doubt that what I teach is [1]sourced in God and not merely [2]my own ideas. *(The preposition [1]ek always points to the source or origin; whereas the preposition [2]apo points away from - both are translated "from" in English. See 2 Corinthians 3:18 and Romans 1:17 See also the use of para in verse 29; which is also translated "from.")*

7:18 He who communicates "[1]away from" his true self pursues his own [2]fame based upon popular opinion - but the one seeking the glory of his Sender *[Source]* finds truth unveiled in their individual I-am-ness and their true righteousness. In this person there is no trace of [3]disharmony! *(Again the preposition [1]apo is used. The word [2]doxa means glory or opinion, here translated fame. The word [3]adikia refers to the system of unrighteousness; which is a system based upon self-righteousness according to personal pursuit and performance as opposed to the righteousness of our redeemed design. The two components of this word are, a, negative and dike meaning two parties finding likeness in each other; this is the stem word for righteousness, dikaiosune.)*

7:19 Did not Moses give you the law whereby you could measure your performance, yet not one of you get it right! I mean what about the "Thou shall not kill" - part? And here you are devising ways on how you can murder me!"

7:20 The people responded with, "You talk like a madman! No one is trying to kill you! You sound like someone with a demon connection rather than a divine one!"

7:21 Jesus answered them, I represent one single poetic expression of the sum total of God's work - compared to the multitudes of rules Moses left you with! And you are astounded at that! *(And still you want to confuse and compare me with Moses! See chapter 6:28-31)*

7:22 Lets take one of those rules: Moses represents circumcision as the tradition of the fathers and you are okay with performing the cut on the Sabbath;

7:23 now in order not to disappoint Moses you have made your circumcision rule superior to the Sabbath; when a boy is eight days old you have no problem with performing circumcision even when it coincides with the Sabbath and here I am making a man's entire body well on the Sabbath and you're ready to kill me and break another one of the ten commandments! *(See Genesis 17:12, "He that is eight days old among you shall be circumcised.")*

7:24 Do not cloud righteous judgment with your biased opinions and traditions."

7:25 The residents in Jerusalem were surprised that Jesus showed up publicly since it was common knowledge that the Jewish leaders sought opportunity to kill him.

7:26 Here he is as outspoken as ever and they are silent! Perhaps they too know deep inside that he is truly the Christ.

7:27 "But then again we know him and his family and are of the opinion that the origin of the Christ was supposed to be a mystery."

7:28 This provoked Jesus to raise his voice passionately while he was teaching in the temple, "You claim to know me and where I come from, yet you fail to recognize that I am not here on my own mission; you clearly show that you do not know him who sent me.

7:29 But I know him for I am his close companion and kinsman; he is the one who sent me." *(Again a different word to the English word "from" See verse 17 - **para**, is a preposition indicating close proximity, a thing proceeding from a sphere of influence, with a suggestion of union of place of residence, to have sprung from its author and giver, originating from, denoting the point from which an action originates, intimate connection - Jesus introduces the Holy Spirit in the same capacity: **parakletos**, meaning close companion, kinsman [John 14:16] - here it is used with **kletos** from **kaleo**, to surname - thus sharing the same family name.)*

7:30 This made them even more determined to seize him yet no one was able to touch him since his hour had not yet come.

7:31 Many in the crowds believed on him and reasoned that no Christ still to come could possibly begin to match the miracles which he already performed.

7:32 The Pharisees were extremely worried when they realized his popularity amongst the people, so with the support of their chief priests they ordered the temple police to arrest him.

7:33 Jesus then said to them, "I will only briefly remain with you where you can see me, then I will be on my way again, [1]sinking out of sight, to be [2]face to face with my Sender. *(The word [1]upago suggests a leading "under" as in under cover. Again John employs the preposition [2]pros.)*

7:34 You will search for me but not find me and where I am your religion cannot take you."

7:35 The Jews couldn't imagine where he would go where they wouldn't find him. Maybe he would join the dispersed Jews and go teach the Gentiles.

7:36 What would he mean by saying that we would seek him and not find him and "where I am you are powerless?"

7:37 On the final day, the crescendo of the eight-day Feast of Tabernacles, Jesus, knowing that he is the completeness of every prophetic picture and promise, cried out with a loud voice, "If anyone is thirsty, let him come and stand [1]face-to-face with me and drink! *(John again employs the word [1]pros in order to emphasize the face-to-face fellowship we are invited into.)*

7:38 In your realizing that I am what the Scriptures are all about, you will discover uniquely for yourself, face to face with me, that you are what I am all about, and rivers of living waters will gush out of your innermost being! *(Jesus addresses the individual; [1]you singular. Here John records how Jesus witnessed the eighth day, the great and final day of the Feast of Tabernacles, when, according to custom, the High Priest would draw water from the Pool of Siloam with a golden jar, mix the water with wine, and then pour it over the altar while the people would sing with great joy from Psalm 118:25-26, See also the entire Psalm 118 which was obviously what Jesus reminded himself of and also Isaiah 12:3; "Therefore with joy shall we draw water from the wells of salvation!" Then, Jesus, knowing that he is the completeness of every prophetic picture and promise, cried out with a loud voice: "If anyone is thirsty, let him come to me and drink! If you believe that I am what the Scriptures are all about, you will discover that you are what I am all about, and rivers of living waters will gush from your innermost being!" The Siloam tunnel is a winding tunnel carved into the rock, leading from the spring of Gihon to the Pool of Siloam. The pool of Siloam also suggests an outflow of waters* שילוח *Shiloach. Dating from the time of Hezekiah [800 BC] or earlier, it was an aqueduct that effectively replaced the Middle Bronze Age channel. Gihon* גחון *derives from,* **Giha** גיח *which means* **gushing forth***; like in an eruption! Also of a child coming forth from the womb. Job 38:8, Psalm 22:9.*

The pool of Siloam as the source in the city of Jerusalem, mirrors your innermost being. When Jesus speaks of waters gushing forth out of your innermost being, he says that you are the city! You are the bride! God's redeemed society! Rev 21:2 And I saw her, in spotless magnificence, the holy city, the new Jerusalem, descending out of the heavens; having been fully prepared as a bride and beautifully adorned for her husband. [In total contrast to the symbolic religious Prostitute city of Babylon.])

7:39 Jesus spoke about the Spirit whom those who would believe that he is the conclusion of Scripture were about to ¹grasp since who Jesus was in all of his majestic splendor was not yet fully acknowledged and thus the Spirit was not yet evident. *(The word often translated, to receive, ¹lambano, means to comprehend, grasp, to identify with. Note, Holy Spirit is an outpouring not an in-pouring!)*

7:40 Many lifted their voices from within the throngs of people and declared that this is indeed the Prophet.

7:41 Others openly announced that he is truly the Christ! Some said, "No this cannot be since he comes from Galilee!

7:42 Scripture clearly states that the Christ is of the seed of David and would be born in David's home town Bethlehem!" *(Micah 5:2; 1 Samuel 16:1)*

7:43 The difference of opinions in the crowd was loaded with tension and divided them.

7:44 Some were eager to arrest him yet no one could touch him.

7:45 At this point the temple police returned to the chief priests and Pharisees who were surprised that they came back empty handed, "Why did you not arrest him?"

7:46 The police officers answered, "We have never heard anyone speak like this before!"

7:47 The Pharisees were shocked, "Are you also deceived?

7:48 Surely we, your leaders should be your informed gauge to what you believe and none of our priests or any of the Pharisees believe in him!

7:49 But these ignorant crowds have no knowledge of the law and are accursed!" *(See Deuteronomy 27:26 "Cursed be everyone who does not abide by all things written in the book of the law, and do them.")*

7:50 Then one of them, Nicodemus, who secretly came to see Jesus earlier, interposed,

7:51 "Does our law condemn someone without first giving them a proper hearing or acquainting ourselves thoroughly with his conduct?

7:52 They sneered at him, "So are you also a Galilean? Search the Scriptures and see for yourself that their is no mention of any future Prophet emerging out of Galilee!" *(Jonah, Hosea, Nahum, possibly also Elijah, Elisha and Amos were from Galilee.)*

Verses 53 and 8:1-11 are not in some of the oldest manuscripts - the reason could probably be that some copyist didn't feel comfortable with this dramatic account - we have no original MSS of the Bible - but thank God for the original authentic Logos and Spirit of Christ resonating in our hearts in the unveiling of Christ in us!

7:53 Everyone went to their homes,

8:1 while Jesus proceeded to the mount of Olives.

8:2 Early dawn he was back at the temple where many people sought to be near him to hear him teach - he sat down and taught.

8:3 Meanwhile the law professors and Pharisees led a woman to him who was forcefully seized in the act of adultery and made her stand in the middle of the throng of people where everyone could stare at her.

8:4 They said unto him, "Teacher, this woman was caught committing adultery.

8:5 Now Moses commanded us in the law that adulterers should be stoned! What would you say?

8:6 They obviously had a clear agenda to snare him in their efforts to build a case of lawlessness against him. Jesus bent down and began to write with his finger on the ground, distracting attention from the girl.

8:7 They continued to interrogate him, then he stood up and looked them in the eyes, *(pros)* and said, "He who is without sin among you, let him cast the first stone at her!"

8:8 And he again bent down and continued writing on the ground.

8:9 They began to walk away one after the other beginning with the oldest. Until Jesus was left alone with the girl, still standing where here accusers dumped her. *("Being convicted by their own conscience" is probably an addition made by some copyist to explain the meaning, which is quite clear without it.)*

8:10 When Jesus stood up again, there was no-one there except the woman. So Jesus asked her, "Where are they? Has no-one condemned you?" *(Where are they, your accusers - your accusers was added by later copyist.)*

8:11 She answered, "No-one Lord!" And Jesus said to her, "Neither am I condemning you - go and sin no more - never again believe a lie about yourself!" *(The word translated sin, **hamartia** from **ha**, negative or without, and **meros**, portion or form; thus distorted pattern - the root of sin is to believe a lie about yourself. See Romans 6:14 Sin was your master while the law was your measure; now grace rules. [The law revealed your slavery to sin; grace reveals your freedom from it. Jesus didn't say to the lady, "Go*

and sin less," he said to her "Go and sin no more!" Jesus knew
something about the life of our design that we had lost sight of! What
he revealed, he also redeemed! Sin –consciousness is what empowers
religion. It always amazes me how Simon could not receive the gift
of the miraculous abundant catch that Jesus blessed him with; he felt
more comfortable with the fact that he caught nothing the previous
night because "I am a sinful man!" He accepted his fate as his due
because his mind was educated under the law of blessings and curses!
[Deuteronomy 28.] When he witnessed the word and the miracle of the
catch, he slotted back into his familiar mode! "Depart from me Jesus! I
am a sinful man! I am not worthy!" Luke 5:8.])

**8:12 And Jesus continued to say, "I am the light of the world -
whoever journeys with me shall not walk in darkness but will
[1]radiate the light of life!"** *(The word [1]echo, to hold; resonate; in this
case, radiate.)*

**8:13 The Pharisees took offence at this and responded with,
"You assume things about yourself; how can you expect us to
believe your record to be true?"**

**8:14 Jesus answered, "Whatever I declare concerning myself is
absolutely true because I know where I am from and where I
am going. You have no clue where I come from and therefore
cannot discern my destiny.**

**8:15 You form your own judgment according to the flesh; I
judge no-one.**

**8:16 And even if I do make a judgment, it is true since I am
not making it up in my imagination or on my own accord, my
reference reflects the testimony of the Father who sent me.**

**8:17 That should settle it for you since it is written in your law
that the testimony of two, is true!** *(This combined witness of two
is not true just because they agree, unless true in fact separately. But
if they disagree, the testimony falls to the ground. Deuteronomy 17:6;
and 19:15. - Robertson. See Heb 6:13-20 and Rev 11:3.)*

**8:18 I am witness to who I am and my Father himself also bears
witness to me.**

**8:19 Then they said to him, "So where is your Father?" And
Jesus answered, "My Father is just as invisible to you as I am
- if you perceived me you would have also seen my Father!"**

8:20 Jesus spoke these words in the temple treasury; yet no-one arrested him since his time was still not due.

8:21 And again Jesus said unto them, "I will go on my way and [1]disappear from your view and you will still seek me, yet die in your [2]sin; your belief-system keeps you trapped in blindfold-mode to make it impossible for you to reach me where I am - your religion is a cul-de-sac!" *(The word [1]upago, to lead under, as in a sinking out of sight, to disappear. The word for sin, [2]hamartia is in the singular, suggesting not sinful acts but rather a condition of a distorted mindset - from ha, negative and meros, portion or form, thus to be without your allotted portion or without form, pointing to a disorientated, distorted identity; the word meros, is the stem of the word morphe, as in 2 Corinthians 3:18 where the word metamorphe, with form, [transform] is the opposite of hamartia - without form. Sin is to live out of context with the blueprint of one's design; to behave out of tune with God's original harmony.)*

8:22 The Jews reasoned that maybe he would kill himself in order to go to a different world because he said, "You cannot come with me."

8:23 Jesus said to them, "You draw your conclusions from the sense ruled world here below - my source points to a different dimension, a realm which is above the horizon of the senses. *(See Colossians 3:1-4.)*

8:24 That is why I said that you will die in your sins because you are not convinced about who I am, you wouldn't know who you are! Your unbelief in my I-am-ness will keep you trapped in this death-ruled dimension, the very dimension that I have come to deliver you from!"

8:25 They asked him again, "Then who are you really?" He answered, "I have told you from the beginning who I am!

8:26 I have many things to say to you and conclude about you in my personal capacity but since you do not believe in me it will mean nothing to you; but he who sent me is true, above your suspicious scrutiny. I speak to the world those things which I have heard from my close companionship with him.

8:27 They just could not make the connection - Jesus' claims about the Father made no sense to their reasoning at all.

8:28 "When you have lifted up the Son of man, *[on the cross of your judgment]* then you will know and understand that I am and that my I-am-ness is demonstrated in my doing; nothing that I do ¹distracts from that; my doing mirrors exactly what my Father has taught me even as my speech reflects his word. *(¹apo, away from, and **emautou** myself. He constantly reminds them of the conclusion of his mission, see 3:14 And as Moses lifted up the serpent in the wilderness, so must the Son of man be lifted up.)*

8:29 And he who sent me on my mission also accompanies me; the Father has never ¹abandoned me for a moment! It is my delight to always do that which ²pleases him. *(¹aphieimi - a word also used for a husband divorcing his wife. The word ²**arestos** to please; it suggests to accommodate one's self to the opinions desires and interests of others.)*

8:30 Whilst listening to him, many were persuaded that he was indeed the Christ.

8:31 Jesus then said to those Jews who were believing in him, "To take my word to its complete conclusion and then to abide in seamless union with its logic is to truly be my disciples. *(Here, he is not referring to some future "red-letter-edition Bible" highlighting his "words"; Jesus is speaking about the Logos defining his "I-am-ness", face to face with God before time was, then documented in prophetic language in ancient Scripture and now unveiled in incarnate human form, as in a mirror.)*

8:32 In this abiding you will fully know the truth about who you are and this knowing will be your freedom.

8:33 They answered him, "We are the seed of Abraham; we have never been anybody's slaves! Why do you suggest that we are not free?"

8:34 Jesus answered and said, "I say unto you with absolute certainty that everyone engaging in the distorted mindset of sin is a slave to it!" *(Sin is not about things you do or don't do - sin is missing out on sonship! Their failing to see Jesus as their Messiah, and him as the mirror image Redeemer of their true sonship, is their sin. Religion is enslaved to the fruit of the wrong tree. The sin-system is governed by the idea of justification by personal effort, performance and pretense; which is the typical fruit of the 'I am-not-mindset' which Peter refers to as the futile ways we inherited from our fathers. 1 Peter 1:18.)*

8:35 The difference between the slave and the son is that the slave only works there; for the son the father's house is home!

8:36 With the freedom found in sonship there is [1]no pretense! *(Free indeed! The word, [1]ontoos, indeed is the opposite to what is pretended.)*

8:37 I know you are the seed of Abraham, yet you are seeking opportunity to kill me because my word finds no [1]resonance in you! *(The word χορός - choros relates to a [1]chorus, harmony in song or dance.)*

8:38 I observe my Father's voice with close attention; this inspires my every expression. You hear a different father's voice and behave accordingly!

8:39 They immediately responded with, "But Abraham is our father!" To which Jesus replied, "If you were conceived by Abraham's faith, you would mirror his persuasion! *(Jesus said in John 6:29 This is the work of God; your belief in the One whom he has sent!)*

8:40 But here you are, desiring to destroy me because I declare to you the truth which I heard from a place of intimate acquaintance with God; this certainly does not reflect Abraham's faith!

8:41 Your actions clearly show who your father is!" They said unto him, "We are not conceived in fornication, God is our only Father!"

8:42 Jesus said, "If you were convinced that God was your Father, you would love me. Look, here I am! I did not arrive here by my own doing; I proceeded from him who sent me!

8:43 You do not understand my [1]language because you do not hear my logic! *(My dialect seems foreign to you because you are not familiar with the Logic of God. You might be acquainted with the letter of the law in Scripture but you are not acquainted with the Word! See John 5:39,40 also John 8:31. The word [1]lalia means dialect or language.)*

8:44 You are the offspring of a perverse mindset and you prove its [1]diabolical parenthood in your willingness to execute its cravings. The intention was to [2]murder humanity's awareness of their god-identity [3]from the beginning since it is in violent opposition to the idea of the image and likeness of God in human form. It cannot abide the truth. Lying is the typical [4]language of the distorted desire of the father of deception. *(The word, [1]diabolos, Devil, has two components, dia, because of, or through and ballo, to cast down; thus referring a cast down condition and warped mentality that mankind inherited in their association with Adam's fall. The diabolos is a man-slayer, [2]anthrōpoktonos from anthropos and kteinoo to kill. The word for the human species, male or female is anthropos, from ana, upward, and tropos, manner of life; character; in like manner. See John 1:51, 2:25. [3]Just like Eve was deceived to believe a lie about herself, which is the fruit of the "I-am-not-tree". The word [4]lalia means dialect or language.)*

8:45 And here I am communicating that which is absolutely true but you are not at all convinced!

8:46 Is there anyone amongst you who can prove me guilty of sin? So if I am telling you the truth, why would you not believe me?

8:47 Whoever realizes their origin in God immediately recognizes the language of God; you do not make that connection since you don't realize your true origin in God!

8:48 The Jews snapped back at him, "We were right all along! You are a Samaritan dog and demon possessed!"

8:49 Jesus answered, "I do not have a demon and I honor my Father while you insult me!

8:50 I am not here to defend my own opinion; God is the judge of my glory.

8:51 Truly, truly do I say unto you, that anyone who treasures my word will not consider death to be of any relevance beyond this age!

8:52 The Jews replied, "Now we are more convinced than ever, that you do have a demon! Abraham and the Prophets died and you say that if someone treasures your word, death will be of no relevance to them unto the age!

8:53 Are you greater than our father Abraham who is dead and the Prophets who are dead? Who do you think you are?"

8:54 Jesus said, "If I honour myself, my honor means nothing; actually it is my Father who honors me, the one you claim to be your God!

8:55 You have never really known him; I know him personally and would lie if I'd say that I haven't seen him! I am not lying like you; I have seen him and treasure his logos! *(Deception is born in the "I am-not" idea)*

8:56 Your father Abraham was leaping with joy to see my day! What he saw made him exceedingly glad!

8:57 Then the Jews said, "Ha! You're not even fifty years old and you claim to have seen Abraham!"

8:58 "Most certainly do I say unto you that before Abraham was born, I am!" *(See note on John 1:1 Three times in this sentence John uses the imperfect of eimi, namely ην aen, to be, which conveys no idea of origin for God or for the Logos, but simply continuous existence, "I am." Quite a different verb egeneto, "became," appears in John 1:14 for the beginning of the Incarnation of the Logos. The incarnation is not the origin of Jesus, neither of us!. See the distinction sharply drawn in John 8:58, "before Abraham was [born, genesthai from ginomai] I am." The word eimi, I am; the essence of being, suggesting timeless existence. See 1 Pet 1:16.)*

8:59 By now they were ready to stone him, but he slipped out of their sight and left the temple area.

9:1 On his way Jesus noticed a man who was born blind.

9:2 And his followers asked him, "Master, whose sin is responsible for this man's condition; is he punished for his own sins, or perhaps for his parent's sins? Why was he born blind?"

9:3 Jesus answered emphatically, "His condition has absolutely nothing to do with any sins committed either by himself or his parents! Neither him nor his parents were guilty of sin, this is an opportunity for God's action *(in Christ)* to be unveiled in him! *(Jesus again disarms the Karma-principle that religion hinges on!)*

9:4 [1]We together, must occupy ourselves to accomplish the work of him who sent me - you must take sides with me! *(John here records a most remarkable statement of Jesus! The best texts read [1]ἡμᾶς, we, instead of ἐμὲ, me/I. Jesus does not say, "I must do the works of him ....". He says, We cannot pull in two opposite directions in the same team! Grace and Karma do not go hand in hand!)*

9:5 The [1]repeated presence of my "I-am-ness" in the world is the light of the world! I am the light of the [2]cosmos!" *(See my commentary on this word in Colossians 3:4, The word, [1]hotan, often translated as "when" is better translated to read "every time." Thus, "Every time Christ is revealed we are being co-revealed in his glory." According to Walter Bauer Lexicon, otan is often used of an action that is repeated. The word, kosmos in the NT refers to the entire human family.)*

9:6 Having said that, he spat on the ground and made clay with the spittle; then he anointed the eyes of the blind man with the clay. *(The clay reminds of the Genesis 2 account of the creation of the earthen vessel of flesh - after the "fall", flesh represents the blindfold-mode, now to be washed off in the waters of spirit dimension.)*

9:7 And said unto him, "Go, and wash in the pool of Siloam. The Hebrew word means outflow. The man went there and washed and returned, seeing perfectly! *(An outflow of waters שילוח Shiloach [Vincent's Word Studies] which reminds of Jesus' urgent announcement at the pool of Siloam on the great day of the feast of tabernacles, "Rivers of living waters will flow out of your innermost being!")*

9:8 The people in the neighborhood and those who knew him before said, "Is this not the blind beggar?"

9:9 Some agreed while others doubted but the he said, "Yes, I am!"

9:10 Then they asked him, "How did it happen that you received your sight?"

9:11 He answered, "A man named Jesus made clay and smeared it over my eyes and said to me to go to Siloam and wash, so I went there and washed and ¹looked up!" (*¹ἀνέβλεψα - aneblepsa means to look up, as in Matthew 14:19 and Mark 16:4*)

9:12 They wanted to know where Jesus was, but the man did not know.

9:13 Then they took him to the Pharisees,

9:14 since it was Sabbath when Jesus made the clay and opened his eyes. (*They knew that the Pharisees would have something to say about their Sabbatical laws that were disregarded by this man Jesus!*)

9:15 The Pharisees demanded to know exactly how it happened that he received his sight. He said, "He put clay on my eyes and I washed and now I see."

9:16 The Pharisees were divided in their opinion; some of them immediately said, "This man cannot be closely associated with God at all since he does not honor the Sabbath. Others were questioning this with, "How can someone who is an obvious sinner according to our law, do such miracles?"

9:17 They then asked the blind man, "So what do you say about this man who opened your eyes?" He said that he thinks Jesus is a Prophet.

9:18 The Jews then began to doubt whether he was blind after all, so they addressed the parents.

9:19 "Is this your son who you say was born blind? How is it that he now sees?"

9:20 The parents said, "Of course we know that this is our son and that he was indeed born blind.

9:21 But how it is that he now sees and who it is who opened his eyes, we have no idea! He is a grown boy, why don't you ask him to speak for himself?"

9:22 They chose their words carefully for fear of offending the Jews since it was rumored that the Jewish leadership agreed to ban anyone from the synagogue should they confess Jesus to be the Christ.

9:23 For this reason the parents didn't want to commit themselves to an opinion but shifted the attention back to the boy himself, saying that he is of age and should be able to speak for himself.

9:24 Then they again called the man that was blind and said to him, "Give God the glory and agree with us that this man is a Sabbath breaker and sinner.

9:25 He said, "I cannot say whether he is a sinner or not, but one thing I do know is that once I was blind but now I see!"

9:26 They wanted to hear it again and asked him, "So what did he do to you, how did he open your eyes?"

9:27 He said, "But I have already told you and you are not hearing me; why would you want to hear it again, are you perhaps also desiring to become his followers?"

9:28 They scorned him and accused him to be a Jesus-disciple! "We are disciples of Moses!

9:29 We know that God communicated with Moses but who can tell where this fellow is from?"

9:30 The man answered them, "I am amazed that you just cannot see this; how can you not perceive where he is from? I mean, hello! He opened my eyes!

9:31 Are we not supposed to know that sinners don't dictate to God - but those who worship God and desires to perform his delight has a "hot-line" to heaven.

9:32 Since the beginning of time no one has ever heard of anyone who opened the eyes of a man born blind!

9:33 If this is not proof of this man's close acquaintance with God, then what is - he would be powerless to perform anything on his own."

9:34 They replied, "You were born in utter sin and here you are trying to teach the saints!" And they cast him out.

9:35 Jesus heard that they cast him out and went looking for him; when he found him, he asked him, "Do you believe in the Son of God?"

9:36 He answered, "Then who is he Sir, that I may believe in him?"

9:37 Jesus said, "You have seen him, and he is speaking to you!"

9:38 And he said, "Lord, I believe. And he worshiped him."

9:39 I have come to judge the world's blindness - so that they who are blind may see and those who think that they see may become blind.

9:40 Some of the Pharisees overheard him and said, "So, are we also blind?"

9:41 Jesus said, "If you were blind you would have no sin, but now you say you see and your sin continues!"

10:1 "I want to make this very clear to you, someone whose agenda is to steal and to plunder the sheep will not come through the gate of the sheepfold; they would climb over the wall or use some other obscure way.

10:2 The shepherd of the sheep enters by the door. *(In the context of Jesus' conversation he emphasizes the fact that the Shepherd-Messiah would surely only enter by the door; which obviously is the familiar voice of the prophetic word.)*

10:3 The gate warden lets him in and the sheep recognize his voice; he calls his sheep by name and leads them out. *(He leads them out of the prophetic enclosure - the fold of safety - into life - where my soul is restored in green pastures! By the waters of reflection my soul remembers who I am - and even if I go through the valley of the shadow of death I will fear no evil - Psalm 23!)*

10:4 And when he leads them out, he goes before them and the sheep follow him; for they are familiar with his voice.

10:5 They will never follow the stranger but flee from him since they do not know his voice."

10:6 Jesus told his disciples this illustration but they did not understand what he meant by it.

10:7 "Let me say it like this then,"Jesus continued, "I am the doorway of the sheep.

10:8 The so-called Shepherds and saviors who preceded me are the thieves and plunderers but the sheep did not recognize their voices.

10:9 I am the door and the sheep who enter because of who I am is safe to roam freely and find pasture.

10:10 The thief "shepherd" has no other agenda but to steal, kill and he couldn't care less if he [1]lost some sheep. I have come with the sole purpose for you to have life in its most complete form. *(The word [1]apolumi, to lose, is often translated to perish - see Luke 15.)*

10:11 I am the shepherd, the good one who lays down his life for the sheep. *(Ez 34:23.)*

10:12 In contrast, the hireling who is not the shepherd and owner of the sheep, sees the wolf approach and leaves the sheep unattended and flees for his life while the wolf kills and scatters the sheep at will!

10:13 The hireling is doing the job merely for the wage and not because of any affection for the sheep.

10:14 I am the shepherd, the good one who knows what is mine and they know me!

10:15 My knowledge of the Father is anchored in his knowledge of me. Because I know my father's heart I lay down my life for the sheep.

10:16 I also have other sheep that are not from this fold; I must lead them too for them to hear my voice and so there will be one flock and one shepherd. *(Second Aorist Active Infinitive of agō with dei expressing the urgency of his mission.)*

10:17 My Father's love is the compelling urgency of my mission which is to lay down my life and receive it again in my resurrection.

10:18 No one takes my life from me, I know who I am when lay it down and from that same place of my I-am-ness, I take it up again. This is the ²conclusion of my Father's prophetic purpose which is what I am all about. *(The word often translated authority or power is the word exousia, from ek + eimi, out of I am. The word ²entole, which is often translated commandment or precept, has two components: en, in and telos, from tello, to set out for a definite point or goal; properly the point aimed at as a limit, that is, by implication, the conclusion of an act or state, the result; the ultimate or prophetic purpose. Strong's 5056 See 1 John 2:3 Mirror Bible.)*

10:19 These words brought more division in their ranks.

10:20 Many of them said that he had a demon and was mad; so, "Why waste your time listening to him?"

10:21 Others said, "These words are definitely not the words of someone with a demon; also, demons do not open the eyes of the blind!"

10:22 Now in Jerusalem they were celebrating the feast of The ¹Renewal of the temple - which was in winter. *(The feast of Renewal, or new beginnings - ἐγκαίνια - egkainia, ¹en + kainos - also known as the Feast of Dedication or the Feast of Lights - which was 3 months after the Feast of Tabernacles - today Hanukkah - meaning to understand, to teach - lasting eight days from the 25th day of Kislev (in December) and commemorating the rededication of the temple in 165 BC by the Maccabees after its desecration by the Syrians. It is marked by the successive kindling of eight lights. It was instituted by Judas Maccabeus, his brothers, and the elders of the congregation of Israel in commemoration of the reconsecration of the Jewish temple in Jerusalem, and especially of the altar of burnt offerings, after they had been desecrated during the persecution under Antiochus Epiphanes (168 BC). This happened on the day, 3 years after the destruction of the temple. The significant happenings of the festival were the illumination of houses and synagogues, and the singing of Psalm 30.*

Jesus lived and communicated from his awareness of the prophetic significance of his life's mission in laying down his life and in co-raising fallen mankind together with him in his resurrection - Hosea 6:2/ Ephesians 2:5. See John 2:19 To which Jesus responded, "The temple will be completely demolished by you and in three days I will raise it up!" See also my commentary note in Mirror Bible.

It is also interesting to note that the numerical value of the name Jesus, is 888 - The name of Jesus in Greek is spelled Ἰησοῦς (iota, eta, sigma, omicron, upsilon, sigma). Substituting in the Greek numeral system the equivalent numerical values to each letter in the name of Jesus and adding them up, the total is 888. The values of each letter are: iota, 10; eta, 8; sigma, 200; omicron, 70; upsilon, 400; sigma, 200. The sum of 10 + 8 + 200 + 70 + 400 + 200 is 888.)

10:23 Jesus was wandering around in the temple in Solomon's porch. *(A covered colonnade on the eastern side of the outer court of the temple - a relic of Solomon's days, which had remained intact in the destruction of the temple by Nebuchadnezzar. Very much in the forefront of Jesus' mind must have been the knowing that at the next Jewish festival - 4 months later - he would fulfil John 1:29 and 2:19 as the Lamb of God to be slaughtered by his own people - for his Father to raise him up on the 3rd day and for mankind to be rebooted into newness of life! En kainos!)*

10:24 Suddenly the Jews closed in on him and demanded to know, "How long will you keep our soul suspended in mid-air? If you are the Christ then tell us plainly!"

10:25 Jesus answered them, "I have told you and you would not believe; all I do is endorsed by my Father and in his name and these works confirm my words."

10:26 Your unbelief shows that you are from a different shepherd's flock, as I've said before. *(You have made deception your shepherd. John 8:38,43,44. John 8:43 You do not understand my language because you do not hear my logic! [My dialect seems foreign to you because you are not familiar with the Logic of God. You might be acquainted with the letter of the law in Scripture but you are not acquainted with the Word! See John 5:39,40 also John 8:31. The word* **lalia** *means dialect or language.])*

10:27 My sheep hear my voice and I know them and they follow me.

10:28 And I give them the life of the ages and they shall never be lost neither shall anyone wrestle them out of my hand.

10:29 As for my Father, what he has given me is most precious and no-one can snatch them out of his hand! *(See Westcott and Hort text [which is more reliable and uses older manuscripts than the Textus Receptus]* ὁ πατήρ μου ὁ δέδωκέν μοι πάντων μεῖζόν ἐστιν. *That which my Father has given me is greater than all. The greatness of the value of the flock, is the ground of their safety. See also Weymouth NT "What my Father has given me is more precious than all besides; and no one is able to wrest anything from my Father's hand.")*

10:30 My Father and I are one!"

10:31 This filled the Jews with renewed rage and they picked up stones to stone him.

10:32 Then Jesus questioned them saying, "I have openly shown you many good works confirming my union with my Father; for which one of these works do you stone me?"

10:33 They said, "We are not stoning you for something that you have done but for what you have just said! You blasphemed God! You are a mere man and you make yourself equal with God? *(The penalty for blasphemy was death by stoning - Leviticus 24:16)*

10:34 Jesus said, "Is it not written in your law, 'I said you are gods?' *(Gen 1:26; Psalm 82:6 All of you are like Elohim since you are* *all sons of the Most High. You are all equal image bearers of the same likeness!)*

10:35 He called them gods, when they encountered the word of God ¹face to face; and the prophetic dynamic of Scripture does not ²dissolve in time! *(Again the word, **pros**, face to face. Scripture cannot be 'broken' - the Greek word is ²**luoo**, to be loosed, or dissolved.)*

10:36 Dare you say of him whom the Father has consecrated and commissioned into the world, "You blaspheme!" because I said that I am the Son of God? *(Sonship implies union with the Father. See Heb 1:1-3. Rev 12:7.)*

10:37 If I was not doing my Father's works then you would have reason not to believe me;

10:38 But if I do, then even if you do not believe me believe the works; then you will understand and be convinced that the Father is in me and I am in him!"

10:39 And again they sought to seize him as they had tried repeatedly in the past, but he escaped out of their hands.

10:40 Meanwhile he went back across the Jordan into the region called Peroea to the place where John first baptized, and remained there.

10:41 Many people followed him saying, "John didn't do any miracles, but everything he said about him is true!"

10:42 And many in that region believed in him.

11:1 Now the brother of Martha and Mary from Bethany was sick.

11:2 This was the same Mary who anointed the Lord with perfumed oil and dried his feet with her hair. *(John looks back from the end of the century as he writes this commentary - even though the anointing is only recorded in chapter 12.)*

11:3 So the sisters sent someone to tell Jesus, "Lord, your dear friend Lazarus is sick."

11:4 His sickness is not to face death but to face the glory of God triumph over and above death! And the Son of God will be glorified because of that. *(The preposition, pros, face to face; and uper, over and above.)*

11:5 Jesus loved Martha, her sister and Lazarus.

11:6 After he heard of Lazarus' sickness he did not go immediately but remained where he was for another two days. *(In his deliberate delay here, again, his mind must have been occupied with his mission - knowing that soon he would enter mankind's death, disengage the gates of Hades and be raised on the third day! See Rev 1:18.)*

11:7 Then he said to his disciples, "Let's go into Judea again."

11:8 His disciples were surprised, "But Master we've just come from there and the Jews wanted to stone you! Now you want to go there again?"

11:9 Jesus replied, "Are there not twelve hours in the day? To walk in the light of day is to walk freely without obstruction.

11:10 But someone who walks in the night would stumble because there is no enlightenment in him.

Seeing-Knowing in the Spirit

11:11 Having said this he added, "Our friend Lazarus is not dead but sleeps and I am going to wake him up out of his sleep."

Seeing + Knowing in Natural

11:12 His disciples responded with, "But Lord if he is only sleeping he should be okay?"

11:13 Yet Jesus meant that his death was nothing more than being asleep but they thought that he meant that he was just taking a rest in a deep sleep.

11:14 So Jesus said it plainly, "Lazarus is dead.

11:15 And for your sakes I am glad that I wasn't there so that you may believe; nevertheless let's go to him."

11:16 Then Thomas said to his fellow disciples, "Let us also go so that we may die with him!" *[Aramaic te'oma meaning twin, or didumos in Greek.]*

11:17 When Jesus arrived Lazarus was already in the tomb for four days.

11:18 Now Bethany was only about two miles from Jerusalem.

11:19 Many Jews came to comfort the two sisters.

11:20 Martha immediately went out to meet Jesus when she heard of his arrival, while Mary was waiting in the house.

11:21 Martha said to Jesus, "Lord, if you'd been here earlier my brother would not have died. *They knew He healed + had the power - But not the depths of His power - still looking @ NAT.*

11:22 But I know that even now whatsoever you would ask of God he will give it to you. *- Martha, Believing but not fully - getting it*

11:23 Jesus said to her, "Your brother shall rise again."

11:24 Martha said, "Yes I know that he shall rise again in the conclusion of time." *She is still only seeing NAT. Not completely* *Going by NAT - not Spiritual*

11:25 Jesus said, "I am the resurrection and the life - he that believes in me shall live even though he died.

11:26 And whoever is alive in the life that I am, shall never die. Do you believe this?"

11:27 Yes Lord, I believe that you are the Christ, the Son of God, who was destined to come into the world.

11:28 Martha then called Mary secretly away from the attention of the mourners, saying, "The Lord is here and he wants to tell you something."

11:29 Mary immediately jumped up and went out quickly to meet him.

11:30 Jesus was not yet in the town where they lived but waited in the place where Martha met with him.

11:31 The Jews who had come from Jerusalem to console her, saw her getting up quickly to leave the house; they thought that she was going to weep at the grave so they followed her.

11:32 When Mary came to the place where Jesus was waiting for her, she fell down at his feet saying to him, "Lord if only you were here, my brother wouldn't have died!"*

91

11:33 When Jesus saw her weeping and also the Jews mourning with her, he groaned in his spirit and was deeply moved.

11:34 He asked, "Where is the tomb?" They said, "Lord come and we'll show you."

11:35 Jesus wept.

11:36 The Jews remarked, "He really loved him very much!"

NAT. eyes + Thoughts

11:37 Some of them reasoned, "Why could this man, who opened the blind eyes of a stranger, not prevent his friend's death?"

11:38 Jesus again groaned in himself as he arrived at the grave; it was a cave with a stone upon it's opening.

11:39 Then Jesus asked for the stone to be taken away. Martha warned that by this time there would be a stench since it was already four days since he passed away.

Still seeing NAT. things-Death

11:40 Jesus answered, "Did I not tell you that in your believing you see the glory of God - *[not in your doubting!] (Believing opens the horizon of your spirit to see beyond the immediate!)*

Thanked the Father!

11:41 Then they removed the stone from the cave where the dead was laid. Jesus lifted up his eyes and said, "Father I thank you that you have heard me.

11:42 I am persuaded that you always hear me; but I am saying this for the sake of those who are standing by so that they too may come to believe that you sent me."

11:43 And after he spoke these words, he raised his voice and hollered, "Lazarus! Come out!"

11:44 And the dead man appeared with his hands and feet swathed in linen cloths also his face was covered in a cloth. Jesus said to them, "Unwrap him and so that he can move around freely."

Signs + Wonders Follow Those Who Believe

11:45 Then many of the Jews who accompanied Mary to the grave believed in him when they witnessed what he just did.

11:46 But some of them went and reported what had happened to the Pharisees.

11:47 The chief priests and Pharisees immediately called a council meeting. "What do we do now? For this man is doing many miracles.

11:48 If we let him alone everyone will believe in him. Then the Romans will come and dispossess us from our land and our national heritage! *(Feeling threatened rather than endorsed in their core identity - thus missing the entire point of the Messiah's mission!)*

11:49 And one of them, Caiaphas who was the High Priest at the time, said, "You don't know what you're talking about.

11:50 If you merely reasoned about this you would have known that it is to our advantage that one should die instead of an entire nation."

11:51 This he said without realizing that in the office of the High Priest he was prophesying Jesus' sacrificial death as the scapegoat of the entire nation.

11:52 And this was not for Israel only but in Jesus laying down his life as the true shepherd of mankind, he would lead together into one family all the children of God from wherever they have been scattered *(into places and circumstances where they have lost their true identity. His death would bring closure to every lie that mankind believed about themselves.)*

11:53 Then from that day they took counsel together to put him to death.

11:54 And so Jesus no longer moved about publicly in Jewish circles. He withdrew into the hill country bordering the desert where he remained with his disciples in the village of Ephraim. *(Near Bethel.)*

11:55 The Jewish Passover was coming up and many people were making their way to Jerusalem to participate in the ceremonial purification before the Easter celebrations.

11:56 Jesus was the topic of conversation among the people in the temple courts. Everyone was curious about his whereabouts and wondered whether he would show up during Passover. *(Passover, or Pasach, פסח protecting and rescuing. From an Arabic root which means to expand; to save. In Ancient Hebrew it is, ☐☀⌐ [reading from right to left, the letter פ pe ⌐ means mouth; then the letter, שׂ or שׂ "s", which means thorn, ☀ - this letter also has the meaning of a shield as thorn bushes were used by the shepherd to build a wall or shield to enclose his flock during the night to protect them from predators. Then, the letter, ☐ for the letter ch, like in the sound, ch in the word, Bach - it is a picture of a tent wall, to protect the occupants from the* *elements outside. Thus, the mouth speaking the prophetic word, announcing the good news of salvation from every possible threat.)*

11:57 The Chief priests and Pharisees *[the Sanhedrin]* **decreed that anyone with information must disclose it so that they can arrest Jesus.** *(They were seeking Jesus six months before at the feast of tabernacles [John 7:11], but now they were ready to kill him.)*

12:1 Six days before Passover Jesus arrived at Bethany where Lazarus whom he raised for the dead lived.

12:2 There they prepared supper for him. Lazarus joined him at the table while Martha was serving them.

12:3 In the meantime Mary took a pound of very expensive spikenard oil and massaged Jesus' feet and wiped it with her hair. The entire house was filled with the fragrance.

12:4 One of his disciples Judas Iscariot, who betrayed him, was shocked at this and said,

12:5 "Why this waste! The perfume could have been sold for a years wages and the money given to the poor!"

12:6 He couldn't care less about the poor! He was a thief and while he was entrusted with the money bag, he would help himself to it!

12:7 Then Jesus said, "Do not hinder her! She has preserved this for the preparation of my burial.

12:8 You will always have the poor to minister to with you but you will not always have me with you.

12:9 A large crowd of Jews heard that Jesus was in Bethany and went there not only to see Jesus but Lazarus who was raised from the dead. *Had to see w/their own eyes.*

12:10 So the chief priests determined to kill Lazarus as well.

12:11 They knew that because of him many were leaving their faith to join Jesus. *- Real heart issues Revealed*

12:12 The following day many people were flocking to the feast because they learned that Jesus was coming to Jerusalem.

12:13 They gathered palm branches and went to meet him while continually [1]shouting Hosea na! His act of rescuing us out of slavery is now realized and celebrated! Well spoken of is the king of Israel who comes in the name of the Lord!" *(The [2]eulogeō, is the well done declaration, connected with the Feast of Tabernacles - Quotation [1]from Psa 118:25, הושע נא na Hosea na! His act of rescuing us out of slavery is now realized and celebrated! Literary, He rescued us! We now recognize and celebrate him! These words were sung by the Jews on the feast of tabernacles, when carrying green branches in their hands, celebrating their deliverance from slavery.*

Also a prophetic reference to Joshua who led them into the promised land! Moses changed his name from Hosea [he saved us] to Yehoshua - Jaweh saved us] pointing to Jesus - יהושע *Numbers 13:16. See note on Luke 1:31.)*

12:14 Having found a young colt, Jesus sat on it and fulfilled that which was written prophetically about him in Scripture.

12:15 Fear not daughter of Sion; rejoice exceedingly! Pay attention! Your king is coming, humbly riding a donkey, a mere colt of a donkey. *(Zec 9:9.)*

12:16 The disciples did not immediately realize the profound significance of this moment; it was only after he was glorified that the full impact of what was written of him and what they did to him dawned on them.

12:17 The people who witnessed the raising of Lazarus from the dead gave testimony to what they have encountered.

12:18 This was also part of the reason why so many people came out to meet him since they too have heard about the miracle.

12:19 The Pharisees were perplexed about this and said, "Look, we are gaining no ground against him! The entire world is running after him!"

12:20 There were also a number of Greeks who came to worship at the feast because of the rumors they have heard.

12:21 They approached Phillip who was from Bethsaida in Galilee and asked him, "Sir, we would be delighted to see Jesus. Is there perhaps any chance that you could introduce us to him?" *(He had a Greek name and the Greeks may have seen Philip in Galilee where there were many Greeks.)*

12:22 Phillip went and told Andrew and the two of them told Jesus.

12:23 Jesus, immediately understanding the prophetic significance of the moment, knew that he, the Messiah, was who all the nations were longing for and answered, "The hour is here for the Son of man to be glorified! *(Jesus studied Scripture as in a mirror - he knew that "in the book, it is written about me!" Haggai 2:7 and the desire of the nations shall come...See Col 1:27.)*

12:24 Most certainly shall the single grain of wheat fall into the earth and die - if it doesn't die it remains alone - but in its death it produces much fruit.

12:25 To hold on desperately to a mere life defined by the soul realm is to lose it; but to abandon the soul substitute for the real deal is to observe your spiritual life which is the life of the ages.

12:26 Whoever continues to minister to me, let him keep on following me; where I go you will share unhindered companionship with me. This shared union is what Father greatly values. *(Note, **ean** with present active subjunctive of diakoneō, keep on serving with dative **emoi**; let him keep on following" - present active imperative of akoloutheō. Literally, **eimi egoo** ... ho emos estai, to be where I am - see John 14:20, In that day you will know that we are in seamless union with one another! I am in my Father, you are in me and I am in you!)*

12:27 My soul is exceedingly perplexed right now! What shall I say, "Father! Rescue me [1]out of the clutches of this hour!" No! This hour is the very culmination of my destiny! *(Greek preposition, [1]ek, out of; source; origin.)*

12:28 "Father! Glorify your name!" And immediately there came a voice out of the heavenly realm saying, "I have glorified it, and I will glorify it again!"

12:29 The crowd heard the voice and said that it had thundered; others thought it was the voice of a celestial messenger.

12:30 Jesus replied, "This voice was not for my sake but for yours! *(Signs are for unbelievers. 1 Corinthians 14:22.)*

12:31 Now is the judgment of this world; this is the moment where the ruler of the world-system is [1]conclusively cast out! *(The serpent's head is about to be crushed! Genesis 3:15; Colossians 2:14,15. This is what the Holy Spirit will convince the world of! John 16:11. John uses a double-barrel word here, **ekballo ekso** - completely thrown out! Thus, taken out of the equation! Luke 10:18.)*

12:32 When I am lifted up from the earth, I will draw all of mankind and every definition of judgment unto me! *(He would be lifted up on a cross, descend into the depths of our hell, then, according to the prophetic word in Hosea 6:2, after two days, the entire human race he represents, will be co-quickened and on the third day, be* *co-raised, out of the lowest parts of the earth and elevated to the highest heavens! Ephesians 4:8,9; see also Ephesians 2:5,6 and Colossians 3:1-3. 'All' includes all of mankind and every definition of judgment. The subject of the sentence, as from the previous verse, is the judgment of the world - thus the primary thought here is that in his death, Jesus would draw all judgment upon himself! John 3:14; John 8:28; Act 2:33. 1 John 3:5 We have witnessed with our own eyes how, in the unveiling of the prophetic word, when he was lifted up upon the cross as the Lamb of God, he lifted up our sin and broke its dominion and rule over us! John 1:29 "Behold, the Lamb of God, who takes away [airo] the sin of the world! The word airo means to lift up.")*

12:33 This he said to point to the way in which he would die. *(See John 19:15 - Lift him up! Lift him up! Crucify him!")*

12:34 The people answered him, "We understood from the law *[the Scriptures]* **that the Christ remains forever. On what basis would you say then, that the Son of man would be lifted up? Who is this Son of man?"**

12:35 Then Jesus said, "Yet a little while the light is in your midst; walk in accordance with the light that you have, *[resonate with; echo]* **then you will not be overtaken by darkness. For the one who walks in darkness has no idea where to go.**

12:36 So long as you have *(echo; resonate)* **the light, live persuaded ¹in the conclusion of light; oh that you ²might realize your authentic origin as the sons of light!** *(The preposition ¹eis points to conclusion; a point reached. The word ²genesthe from ginomai, to be born, to become is in the Aorist Subjunctive Mood, which is similar to the Optative expressing a wish. The Mood of the Greek verb expresses the mode in which the idea of the verb is employed. This wish is consistent with the theme of John's conversation in this book, see John chapter 1. See also 2 Peter 1:19 For us the appearing of the Messiah is no longer a future promise but a fulfilled reality. Now it is your turn to have more than a second-hand, hear-say testimony. Take my word as one would take a lamp at night; the day is about to dawn for you in your own understanding. When the Morning Star appears, you no longer need the lamp; this will happen shortly on the horizon of your own hearts.*

To walk in the light as he is in the light means to see your life and everything that concerns you, exclusively from your Father's point of view. You are indeed the focus of your Father's attention and affection. To be convinced of your origin in God and Father's initiative in redeeming your mind from all the lies you believed about yourself, is the vital energy of the law of liberty. To reflect the opinion of God in your attitude and conversation makes your life irresistibly attractive.)

12:37 Even though he had done so many miracles in front of their eyes they were still not persuaded about him.

12:38 Their persistent unbelief reminds of what Isaiah said, "Lord, who has believed our report? To whom has the arm of the Lord been revealed! Who understands how God has reached into our world?

12:39 They were incapable of faith since Isaiah also said,

12:40 "He has blinded their eyes and hardened their heart so they cannot see with the eyes nor perceive with the heart and be transformed where I shall heal them." *(See Romans 9:17-33; also 11:7 The very thing Israel sought to obtain through their diligent labor they failed to get; yet those who embraced grace as God's original intent hit the bull's eye every time, leaving the rest groping around in the dark like blindfolded archers.*

Romans 11:8 Isaiah said that God has given them a spirit of slumber, causing their eyes and ears not to function. This drowsiness seems to prevail even to this day. [Unbelief and religious ritual are blindfolds. "And the Lord said, this people draw near to me with their mouth and honor me with their lips but remove their hearts and minds far from me, and their fear and reverence for me are a commandment of men that is learned by repetition ... ." Isa 29:10 - 24])

12:41 Isaiah said these things when he saw the beauty of God on exhibit in the Messiah. *(And he could not understand that the people of Israel wouldn't see this for themselves!)*

12:42 Many of the chief rulers believed that Jesus was the Messiah but because of the Pharisees they would not openly confess him since they knew that they would be thrown out of the synagogue.

12:43 They loved the [1]opinion and recognition of people more than the opinion of God. *(The word often translated, glory, [1]doxa from dokeo, to form an opinion.)*

12:44 Jesus cried out and said, "To believe in me is not proof that I won your vote; it proves your belief in the one who sent me!

12:45 To see me is to see him who sent me.

12:46 I have come to enlighten the world so that anyone who believes in me should no longer abide in darkness.

12:47 If any one hears my words and rejects them, I do not judge that person; for I did not come to judge the world but to save the world!

12:48 The one who rejects me and my words has one who judges him, the very Word that I have spoken to him is the final judge. No-one will escape the ultimate scrutiny of the Word!

12:49 I have not conjured up what I have spoken to you but the Father who sent me has given me specific instruction to say what I do in the way that I do it.

12:50 And I know that this instruction is the life of the ages - the detail of what I say echoes exactly what I've heard my Father say.

13:1 Now Jesus having known, before the feast of the Passover, that this was his hour; he knew very well that he would step out of this world into his Father's embrace. *[pros - face to face.]* He drew much love-energy from his own who would remain still in the world after his departure; He loved them completely. *(Passover, or Pasach, פסח protecting and rescuing. From an Arabic root which means to expand; to save. See John 11:56.)*

13:2 It was supper time and the [1]diabolos already had the heart of Judas Iscariot in sync with his own, which was to betray Jesus. *(During supper - deipnou ginomenou, which is the correct text, present middle Participle of ginomai - [not genomenou, second Aorist middle Participle, "being ended"] The [1]devil, dia because of and ballo, cast down; because of the fall; referring to the fallen mindset - the one that will be crushed by the Seed of the woman - 'put into the heart of Judas, 'ballo eis kardia'... thus Judas' heart was in sync with the fallen mindset.)*

13:3 Jesus was fully aware of the fact that his Father has given all things into his hands; he knew that he came from God and that his destiny was to return face to face with God. *(As the incarnate word he knew that he is the exhibit of the thoughts of God in human form; he knew that he fulfilled what Isaiah saw when he spoke about the thoughts of God that would come down from heaven like rain and snow to saturate the earth, making it bring forth and sprout, giving seed to the sower and bread for food, before it returns again to heaven. "So shall my word be, that proceeds from my mouth, it shall not return to me empty but prosper in my purpose!" He has come to mirror God's mind towards mankind.)*

13:4 So he got up from the table and took off his outer garments and wrapped a towel around him.

13:5 He then poured water into a basin and began to wash the feet of his disciples and dried them with the towel around his waist.

13:6 When he came to Simon Peter, he protested saying, "Lord do you want to wash my feet?"

13:7 Jesus answered, "You might not appreciate it now but afterward you will understand the significance of what I am doing!"

13:8 Peter refused and said, "I will never allow you to wash my feet!" And Jesus replied, "If I do not wash you then you have no participation with me."

13:9 Then Peter said, "Lord, not only my feet but also my hands and head!"

13:10 But Jesus answered, "He that has already taken a bath only needs to wash his feet for he is completely clean. And you are already clean, yet not everyone of you."

13:11 For Jesus knew who would betray him - that is why he said, "you are not all equally clean." *(Not all of you have given the word the same opportunity to wash your minds! According to custom the guest was supposed to bathe [louō] before coming to a feast and so only the feet had to be washed [niptō] on removing the sandals.)*

13:12 So when he was done he put his robe back on again and reclined at the table and asked them, "Do you understand what I just did?

13:13 You call me your Instructor and Lord and its good, for so I am;

13:14 If I, your teacher and Lord have washed your feet; you too ought to wash one another's feet!

13:15 For I have demonstrated an example for you to mirror.

13:16 For I would want you to know most certainly that the servant is not greater than his Lord and the one sent is not greater than the one who sent him.

13:17 To know these things is to find your joy in expressing them in your lifestyle.

13:18 I am not talking about all of you; I have chosen you and know that one of you will kick me like a horse, just as it is written, 'Even my trusted friend, who ate bread with me has turned his heel against me.' *(Psalm 41:9 In Greek literature the metaphor is of one administering a kick. Thus Plutarch, describing the robber Sciron, who was accustomed "out of insolence and wantonness to stretch forth his feet to strangers, commanding them to wash them, and then, when they did it, with a kick to send them down the rock into the sea!")*

13:19 I'm telling you this in advance so when it happens you may be persuaded about me.

13:20 I also assure you that whoever can [1]identify with your mission, identifies with me and therefore identifies with him who he sent me." *(The word ¹lambano, means to take to oneself, to comprehend, grasp, to identify with.)*

13:21 Having said this Jesus was again deeply disturbed in his spirit and said, "I am telling you now that one you is about to betray me!"

13:22 The disciples were confused, looking at one another and wondering who this person could possibly be.

13:23 One of the disciples was leaning against the bosom of Jesus, cuddled up in his love;

13:24 Simon Peter prompted him to ask Jesus who it was.

13:25 So he did, "Jesus, who is it?"

13:26 Jesus relied, "It is the one I'll give the morsel of bread to once I have dipped into the broth." He then dipped the morsel and handed it to Judas Iscariot, Simon's son.

13:27 Wrapped up in that morsel was the opportunity for Satan to now fully engage the mind of Judas. Then Jesus said to Judas, "Do what you've got to do and get it over and done with ." *(Literally, ¹meta, together with the morsel...)*

13:28 Even now the other disciples did not suspect Judas in the least. *(Amazing how Jesus never treated Judas any differently even though he knew that he was stealing money from them.)*

13:29 Some thought that since Judas was their treasurer Jesus asked him to go and buy necessities for the feast, or perhaps to go and give some money to the poor.

13:30 With that, Judas left immediately; and it was night.

13:31 Then, with Judas gone, Jesus said, "This seals the glorification of the Son of man, as well as God's glorification in him.

13:32 In this joint glorification God is glorified in himself - In God glorifying mankind in himself, his personal glory is not diminished at all, but fully endorsed! This is happening immediately and seamlessly! *(Whatever God accomplished in Jesus the incarnate Christ is of immediate consequence to the human race.)*

13:33 Little children, I am with you for a very little while, then you will seek me, but as I said to the Jews, where I go you cannot join me; so now I say to you,

13:34 I give you a new commandment, keep on loving one another just as I have loved you - my love for you is the source of your love for one another. *(The word èntole, which is often translated commandment or precept, has two components: en, in and telos, from tello, to set out for a definite point or goal; properly the point aimed at as a limit, that is, by implication, the conclusion of an act or state, the result; the ultimate or prophetic purpose. Strong's 5056.)*

13:35 In this environment of your love for one another everyone will come to know your discipleship unto me.

13:36 Simon Peter then asked him, "Lord, where are you going?" Jesus answered, "Where I am about to go, you are not able to accompany me right now, but you will afterwards. *(See 14:1 I go to prepare a place for you that where I am you may be also!)*

13:37 Peter said, "But Lord, why cannot I follow you right now? I will give my life for you!"

13:38 Jesus said, "Will you give your life for me? I say to you now, most certainly will you have contradicted me three times before the cock crows."

14:1 Set your troubled hearts at ease by letting your belief [1]conclude in God as you rest your confidence in me. *(The preposition[1]eis, means a point reached in conclusion.)*

14:2 What makes my Father's house home, is your place in it! If this was not the ultimate conclusion of my mission why would I even bother to do what I am about to do if it was not to prepare a place for you? I have come to persuade you of a place of seamless oneness where you belong. *(See John 8:35 The difference between the slave and the son is that the slave only works there; for the son the father's house is home! 8:36 With the freedom found in sonship there is [1]no pretense! [Free indeed! The word, [1]ontoos, indeed is the opposite to what is pretended.] What Jesus is about to accomplish in his death and resurrection will forever shift the idea of religious works and pretense and performance from the typical slave-mentality to the freedom and reality of sonship!)*

14:3 The proportions of what I will accomplish are astonishing! I will [1]prepare a highway for you, just as in the Oriental custom, where people would go before a king to level the roads to make it possible for royalty to journey with ease and comfort. Then I will personally come to escort you on this royal highway, guiding you to be where I am, in seamless, face to face oneness in the Father's embrace. [v 20] By [2]fully identifying myself with you I have mirrored you in me so that you may be completely at home where I am! *(Jesus sees the full scope of his work: by submitting himself to our judgment and hellish fury, he would enter our death and gloom and thereby strip every principality and dominion of its judgment and power-play over the human race. Colossians 2:14,15. The word [1]hetoimazō suggests a levelling of the road to make it passable for kings! [Isaiah 40:3-5] The word [2]paralambano, carries two components, para, a preposition indicating close proximity, a thing proceeding from a sphere of influence, with a suggestion of union of place of residence, to have sprung from its author and giver, originating from, denoting the point from which an action originates, intimate connection; and lambano, to comprehend, grasp, to identify with. He would lead us in his triumphant procession on high out of our darkness into his marvellous light, where we may now participate in the union of the ages - "and take you to myself so that you may be where I am, face to face with the Father!" Hosea 6:2; Ephesians 4:8; Colossians 1:13. John 1:1,2. See John 1:18 Until this moment God remained invisible; now the authentic, incarnate begotten Son, the blueprint of our design who represents the innermost being of God, the Son who is in the bosom of the father, brings him into full view! He is the official authority qualified to announce God! He is our guide who accurately declares and interprets the invisible God within us.)*

Knowing

14:4 In fact, you [1]have always known this way and where all this is leading me and where I am taking you. *(The word, οιδατε oidate, is the Perfect Active tense of eido, to see; to perceive. The Perfect Tense denotes an action which is completed in the past, but the effects of which are regarded as continuing into the present. Jesus here appeals to a different level of knowing - not a mere academic knowing but a deep inner knowing, a remembering like in Psalm 22:27.)*

14:5 Thomas said, "No, we don't get it; we have no idea where you are going with this - how could we possibly have known the way?"

14:6 Jesus said, "My I-am-ness *[mirrored in you]* **is your way; this is your truth and also your life! Every single person [1]is now brought face to face with the Father entirely because of my doing."** *(The verb ἔρχομαι erchomai, is in the Present tense and the Passive voice - ερχεται erchetai - which makes the subject the recipient of the action!)*

14:7 If you had known me for who I really am, you would have immediately recognized my Father in me. Now, with me bringing you back face to face with the Father, you will certainly know him and [1]become fully acquainted with him. *(The word [1]horao implies encounter.)*

14:8 Phillip said to him, "Lord, [1]show us the Father, then we will be satisfied." *([1]Aorist imperative - denoting aspect, not tense; once and for all.)*

14:9 "Phillip, I have been with you for a long time, and yet you haven't really known me? To see me is to see the Father! How can you still say, "Show us the Father?" *(Phillip was the one who introduced Nathaniel to Jesus in the beginning of their walk with him. "We have found him of whom Moses and the Prophets wrote!" John 1:46. The Father cannot appear in any more visible or tangible manner than what he did in Jesus, the incarnate Word. Any idea one could possibly have about God that is unlike Jesus, is not the Father! He is the radiant and flawless expression of the person of God. He exemplifies the character and every attribute of God in human form. Hebrews 1:3; Colossians 1:15.)*

14:10 Are you not convinced that I am in the Father and that the Father is in me? We are in seamless union. The words that

I speak to you are not my independent opinion or ideas; the Father in me addresses you; this conversation then translates into the Father's action unveiled in my doing.

14:11 The fact that the Father seems distant or invisible to you does not mean that he is absent. In me he is very present with you! You cannot claim to know me while you ignore him - we are inseparable. I dare you *[plural]* to believe that I am in the Father and the Father in me - if it seems far fetched, then believe me because of what I have done and what I am about to do. It is the Father in me who defines me. My works exhibit his resolve. *(Jesus does not have to persuade the Father about us, he came to persuade us about the Father. There is nothing in the incarnate Word that is in conflict with who God is! John 1:1-3 If you underestimate me, you underestimate my Father - and you underestimate you!)*

14:12 I want you to be fully convinced about this, anyone whose belief concludes in who I am, will also do the works that I do. And because of my [1]relocation to continue to be [2]face to face with my Father, my works will be greatly multiplied through you; the Father is as present in you as he is in me. *(The word, [1]poreuomai, to transfer, relocate, to travel. Again the word, [2]pros, face to face. Jesus is multiplied in us.)*

14:13 And whatever you desire in my name, that will I do that the Father may be glorified in the Son. Your sonship is endorsed in my sonship. *(The first occurrence of the phrase, In my name, en tōi onomati mou. See also John 14:26; 15:16; 16:23, 16:24, 16:26. "If this name, Jesus Christ is in the believer's consciousness, the element in which the prayerful activity moves; so that thus that Name, embracing the whole revelation of redemption, is that which specifically measures and defines the disposition, feeling, object, and contents of prayer. The express use of the name of Jesus therein is no specific token; the question is of the spirit and mind of him who prays" Meyer.)*

14:14 If you ask me anything, in knowing what my name entitles you to, that will I perform. *(The use of 'me' here is supported by Aleph B 33 and the Vulgate Syriac Peshitta manuscripts. Aleph is the famous Sinaiticus, the great discovery of Constantine von Tischendorf, the only surviving complete copy of the New Testament written prior to the ninth century; [4th century].)* Manuscripts

14:15 In your loving me you will greatly value and treasure [1]the prophetic conclusion of my ministry. *(The word [1]entole, which is often translated commandment or precept, or assignment, has two* components, *en*, in and *telos*, *from tello*, to set out for a definite point or goal; properly the point aimed at as a limit, that is, by implication, the conclusion of an act or state, the result; the ultimate or prophetic purpose. Strong's 5056. See 1 John 2:3.)

14:16 In my prayerful engagement with the Father, he will give you [1]**another** [2]**close companion to be with you - in such an intimate way that** [3]**my immediate presence will continue to be** [4]**inseparably one with you in** [5]**timeless ages to come!** *(The word allos is used here. The words* [1]*allos and heteros are both usually translated as "another" in English. Yet allos means "another of the same kind" and heteros means "another of a different type". The word,* [2]*parakaleo, alongside, closest possible proximity of nearness; and kaleo, to identify by name, to surname. Also, kinsman; intimate companion. See Rom 12:8. "...just be there alongside someone to remind them of their true identity." 1 Thessalonians 5:11 Continue, as you so eloquently do, to edify one another by cultivating the environment of your close association in your joint-genesis. [The word parakaleo is here translated as our joint-genesis] The words, ina he meth [meta] umoon eis ton aiona he - ινα η μεθ υμων εις τον αιωνα - the verb* [3]*he from eimi, I am, is in the Present Active Subjunctive form, to continue to be;* [4]*meta, with, inseparably one with you in* [5]*aiona, the timeless ages!)*

(In the left margin:) Another of the ~ Same Kind

14:17 Your eternal companion is the Spirit of truth, whom those trapped in the sense-ruled world, just cannot [1]**get to grips with! Their visual horizon is veiled, and they are unable to understand what they cannot see. But,** *[in your acquaintance with me],* **you are familiar with this** [2]**seamless, intimate union, and the Spirit's continued presence within you.** *(The word,* [1]*lambanoo, to grasp; to get to grips with. The following 3 verbs are all in the Present Active Indicative tense, which is the timeless present tense, and indicates continued action, something that happens continuously or repeatedly, or something that is in the process of happening: to know, ginosko; to abide meno; and to be eimi. Thus,* [2]*ginooskete, a knowing that is extended beyond the moment. The "absence" of Jesus will not interrupt this knowing. [See verse 20!] Then, ότι παρ' ὑμῖν μένει hoti because, para, closest possible nearness and intimate acquaintance, and* [2]*meno - to abide in seamless oneness; and is present in you! καὶ ἐν ὑμῖν ἐστίν kai en humin estin- the Spirit already resides in you. In the Incarnate Word, spirit dimension is not a foreign place, neither is the Spirit a foreign person to you!)*

14:18 At no time will you be orphaned or abandoned by me; I come to abide [1]face to face with you. *(I come to be no less face to face with you than what I've always been face to face with the Father from the beginning for all eternity. The Holy Spirit does not replace but reinforces the presence of Jesus and the closeness of the Father. Again, John uses the word [1]pros, face to face. See John 1:1)*

14:19 In yet a little while and the world will no longer see me but I will be tangibly visible to you in the very life we share together.

14:20 In that day you will know that we are in seamless union with one another! I am in my Father, you are in me and I am in you! *(The incarnation does not divide the Trinity; the incarnation celebrates the redeemed inclusion of humanity! Picture 4 circles with the one fitting into the other - The outer circle is the Father, then Jesus in the Father, then us in Jesus and the Holy Spirit in us! This spells inseparable, intimate oneness! Note that it is not our knowing that positions Jesus in the Father or us in them or the Spirit of Christ in us! Our knowing simply awakens us to the reality of our redeemed oneness! Gold does not become gold when it is discovered but it certainly becomes currency!)*

14:21 Whoever [1]resonates and [2]treasures the [3]completeness of my prophetic purpose cannot but fall in love with me and also find themselves to be fully participating in my Father's love and I will love this one and make myself distinctly known and real to each one individually. In this embrace of inseparable union love rules! *(Intimacy is not the result of suspicious scrutiny but the inevitable fruit of trust! [1]Echo, to have; to hold; to resonate. The word, [2]tereo, means to treasure ; to safeguard. The word [3]entole, which is often translated commandment or precept, or assignment, has two components, en, in and telos, from tello, to set out for a definite point or goal; properly the point aimed at as a limit, that is, by implication, the conclusion of an act or state, the result; the ultimate or prophetic purpose. Strong's 5056.)*

14:22 Judas, not Iscariot, said to him, "Lord, how is it that you will make yourself visible to us and not to the world?" *(This is the fourth interruption of the talk of Jesus: by Peter, 13:36; by Thomas, 14:5; by Philip, 14:8; and now by Judas.)*

14:23 Jesus answered, "This is so much more than a mere casual, suspicious or indifferent observation, whoever loves me will treasure my words and know my Father's love and we will come face to face with this one and make our abode with

#3438

[para] each one individually." *(We will make our abode, [1]mone, the same Greek word that is rendered mansions in the KJV in the former part of this chapter. God doesn't dwell in buildings made by human hands - God has no other address but 'you'-man life!)*

14:24 To be indifferent to me and my words is to be equally indifferent to my Father's word; and I am commissioned by him.

14:25 This has been my constant conversation with you in our time together.

14:26 The Holy Spirit is about to become your close companion, sent by my Father in my name to represent me, to teach you all things and remind you of everything that I have spoken to you. Thus my word will continue to find a voice in you.

14:27 Peace be with you! I give you my own peace - this is not the kind the world gives - this is peace in the midst of troubled times; therefore you have nothing to fear! Let not your hearts be timid.

14:28 You have heard me say that I go away to come to be face to face with you; now if you're in love with me you would not be threatened by the idea of my departure, but you would rejoice since I'll be going to the Father and my Father is greater than me. From now on we will be present in a much closer capacity to you than what I could ever be while I am with you in the flesh!

14:29 What I now tell you is to prepare you for what is about to happen, so that when it happens, you will not be shaken in your belief but stand strong.

14:30 In my going *[into your judgment,]* my silence should not disturb you; *[like a lamb led to slaughter, he opened not his mouth]* the ruler of this world-order comes but this "voice" has nothing in common with mine - there is no [1]resemblance or resonance! *(The word [1]echo, to have, to hold, to resonate.)*

14:31 Thus the world will understand my love for my Father and it will be clear to them that I have accomplished his [1]prophetic purpose. Arise, let's go! *(See note in 14:15 for [1]entelomai. They rose from the table, left the city, and went towards the garden of Olives, or garden of Gethsemane, on the road to which, a part of the following discourse was delivered. It was now about midnight, and the moon was almost full, it being the 14th day of her age, about the time in which the Jewish Passover was to be slain. Adam Clark.)*

110

15:1 I am the authentic ¹vine! My Father is the farmer. *(The word* ¹*ampelos, grapevine; from amphi, around and halōn, from the base of heilissō, to roll up or together; thus a vine coiling about a support. "On the Maccabean coinage Israel was represented by a vine". Jesus is the genuine Messianic vine. Robertson. Not the empty vine Hosea 10:1 mentions. See also Matthew 21:33.)*

15:2 Every offshoot in me that does not bear fruit, he ¹lifts up from the ground and fastens it to the stake and every fruit bearing part he ²dresses in order to maximize its yield. *(The words* ¹*airei and* ²*kathairei are employed to suggest the lifting of the branches as well as the dressing process which includes pruning.* ***Airei,*** *from* ***airoo, to elevate, to lift up, to air;*** ***katharei,*** *from* ***kata,*** *in this case signifying intensity, and again* ***airoo.*** *[Lifting up to manage a* ✕ *grape vine's canopy which will influence not only the potential yield of the crop but also the quality of the grapes due to the access of air and sunlight needed for the grapes to ripen fully and for preventing various grape diseases.] When the Greeks began to colonize southern Italy in the 8th century BC, they called the land Oenotria which could be interpreted as "staked" or land of staked vines, growing upwardly. The grapevine is attached to stakes, or posts, thus making sure the branches grow upwardly. They are also dressed and pruned to be positioned in such a way that their fruit would be easily accessible.* ***Hina karpon pleiona pherēi,*** *purpose clause with* ***hina*** *and present active subjunctive of* ***pherō,*** *"that it may keep on bearing more fruit" (more and more). The Father's vineyard tool is his Word, incarnated in* ~~EXCELLENT~~ *sonship; as in Hebrews 1:1-3 and Heb 4:12. Hebrews 1:1 Throughout ancient times God spoke in many fragments and glimpses of prophetic thought to our fathers. Heb 1:2 Now, the sum total of this conversation with us, has finally culminated in a Son. In his sonship, God declares him heir of all things. He is, after all, the author of the ages. Heb 1:3 Jesus is the crescendo of God's conversation with us; he gives context and content to the authentic thought. Everything that God had in mind for mankind is voiced in him. Jesus is God's language. Jesus is the radiant and flawless expression of the person of God. He makes the glorious intent of God visible and mirrors the character and every attribute of God in human form. Heb 4:12 The message God spoke to us in Christ, is the most life giving and dynamic influence in us, cutting like a surgeon's scalpel, sharper than a soldier's sword, piercing to the deepest core of human conscience, to the dividing of soul and spirit; ending the dominance of the sense realm and its neutralizing effect upon the human spirit. In this way mankind's spirit is freed* *cont.*

to become the ruling influence again in the thoughts and intentions of the heart. The scrutiny of this word detects every possible disease, discerning the body's deepest secrets where joint and bone-marrow meet. (The moment we cease from our own efforts to justify ourselves, by yielding to the integrity of the message that announces the success of the Cross, God's word is triggered into action. What God spoke to us in sonship (the incarnation), radiates his image and likeness in our redeemed innocence.) [Heb 1:1-3] This word powerfully penetrates and impacts our whole being; body, soul and spirit.)

15:3 Your personal pruning and dressing already happened in our conversation; The word made flesh in my person and language is how the Father prepares and sets you up for fruit bearing.

15:4 Our seamless union, you in me and I in you, is pictured in the vine: the shoot cannot bear fruit outside of this union. In its abiding in the vine, fruit happens naturally - as with your abiding in me.

15:5 I am the vine and you are the branches; it is the one who understands this mutual union that naturally bears much fruit - which is impossible to happen apart from me.

15:6 [1]Every area of human life that does not continue to be entwined in this place of seamlessness in me, [2]was already cast forth where it has [3]withered away and is gathered to be burned as [4]firewood. *(The word [1]tis is an enclitic indefinite pronoun; some or any person or object. So, instead of 'everyone' I chose to see tis here as referring to everything, meaning every area of your life. As mentioned in verse 2, the 'dressing' or 'pruning' is not in judgment but in order to maximize the yield! God's faith sees mankind fully associated, included*
✷ *and represented in the incarnation. He called things which were not yet visible as though they were, because they are! Romans 4:17! "When God changed Abram's name to Abraham, he made a public statement that he would be the father of all nations. (Genesis 17:5) Here we see Abraham faced with God's faith; the kind of faith that resurrects the dead and calls things which are not (visible yet) as though they were." Human failure in every tense and sense of the word was dealt with in Jesus death, burial and resurrection. The Aorist Passive tense, [2]eblethe, denoting a momentary act in the past tense, indicates that it was cast forth. The next verb is also in the Aorist Passive, [3]exeranthe, it was withered away, from xerainoo, to wither. The incarnate Christ is*

about to enter into mankind's judgment and hell and bear the ultimate victorious fruit in co-raising us together with him. The single grain of wheat did not abide alone but bore much fruit! John 12:24. See also 12:31 and 32, This is the judgment of this world; it is the moment where the authority of the world-system is cast out! [The serpent's head is about to be crushed! Genesis 3:15; Colossians 2:14,15] See Colossians 3:1 Engage your thoughts with your co-crucifixion and co-resurrection and co-seatedness in Christ! And 12:32 When I am lifted up from the earth, I will draw all judgment unto me! [4]*From living fruit-bearing branches to firewood, which becomes recycled energy again! See Extended Commentary Notes after the final chapter of the Mirror - Thoughts on Judgment and Resurrection.)*

15:7 My words find voice in you. With your abiding in me and my words abiding in you a conversation is inspired where you will request that which arises in your desire from our union and it shall come to pass for you!

15:8 These union-inspired desires bear the very fruit that endorses the Father's glory! This is where true discipleship is born. *(The Aorist tense; was glorified. As in Joh 15:6, marking the point when the Father's glory was realized in the perfect union of the believer's will with Christ's.)*

15:9 The love of the Father for me is my love for you - abide in my love for you!

15:10 By [1]**treasuring the** [2]**Prophetic conclusion of my life you will remain constantly engulfed in my love even as I treasure the completeness of my Father's prophetic purpose and abide in his love embrace.** *(*[1]*tereo, to treasure, to guard; entole, see note in 14:15.)*

15:11 I have spoken these things unto you so that my joy will continuously infuse you - you don't have to invent your own if you can tap into mine! This is the ultimate bliss!

15:12 I [1]**advise you to discover your love for one another mirrored in my love for you; this is the** [1]**conclusion of my mission.** *(The word often translated assignment or commandment,* [1]*entole, from en in and telo, complete. See note in John 14:15.)*

15:13 There is no greater expression of love than the love that leads someone to lay down his life for his friends. *("Self-sacrifice is the high-water mark of love." Dods)*

15:14 Our friendship is endorsed in your continual engagement with ¹the conclusion of my mission. *(Again the word ¹entole, assignment or conclusion.)*

15:15 I do not communicate with you on a slave - boss basis; slaves have no clue what their Master is about to do. I talk to you as my friends telling you everything that I have heard in my conversation and ¹intimate association with my Father. This I explain to you in the ²clearest possible terms. *(The preposition ¹para is used here, pointing to close companionship; the word ²gnoritso means to have thorough knowledge of.)*

15:16 I did not begin in you; you began in me! I am not your idea; you are mine! I have strategically positioned you in order that you may abound in much fruit bearing, wherever life leads you - fruit that would ceaselessly continue this same incarnate life of union with me! From within this place, anything you desire has already been granted you by my Father. *(The word, ¹eklegomai, traditionally associated with the idea of election, has two components, ek, a preposition that indicates source or origin and lego, meaning to communicate ideas; thus, the original blueprint-word, the logos; see John 1:1-3 and 12. The word becomes flesh in the fruit you eat! The many are called, [kaleo] but few are "chosen" eklegomai thus, The masses are defined by my name but few realize their origin in me!)*

15:17 All these things are the conclusion of my assignment to you and find their context in your love for one another.

15:18 Know that the world-system hated me first whenever you encounter their resistance against you.

15:19 If your lives were the product of the world-system you would enjoy their ¹applause and friendship; but they can't stand you because their mold no longer has any hold on you, now that you have discovered your authentic identity in my ²declaration of who you are by design. *(¹Phileo, friendship. Again the word ²eklegomai is used. See 3:31 We are dealing with two dimensions here, the one coming from above presides over all - while the reasoning from a mere earthly perspective is confined to communicate from an earthly point of view. The conversation realized as originating in heaven has the final say. Also 3:13 No one can fully engage in heaven's perspective, unless one's heavenly origin is realized! The Son of man declares mankind's co-genesis from above!)*

15:20 Remember that I told you that within the environment and association of servant and Master, what happens to the Master happens also to the servant - the servant is not treated any differently - if they hunted me down, they will hunt you down; if they treasured my word they would also treasure yours.

15:21 They will do all these things unto you because of your association with me, since they have no regard for him who sent me.

15:22 My arrival and my conversation, *[the logos becoming flesh]* removed any possible excuse of ignorance they could have had to continue in a distorted pattern of life. In my absence they would have had no sin, but now they have no valid excuse.

15:23 To dishonor me is to dishonor my Father.

15:24 If I had not accomplished in them the works which nobody else has ever performed they would have had reason to remain trapped in their distorted pattern of life; yet, in spite of what they have witnessed with their own eyes, they continue to despise my Father and I.

15:25 Their hatred for me fulfils the word of their own law. *(As recorded in Psalm 69:4, They that hate me without a cause and in Psalm 35:19 Let not those rejoice over me who are wrongfully my foes, and let not those wink the eye who hate me without cause.)*

15:26 But when the close Companion comes, who I shall send to you from the immediate presence of the Father, the Spirit of the truth who originates and proceeds out of the Father, this One will confirm everything about me.

15:27 You also will confirm everything about me since you are with me from the beginning. *(You now know your joint I-am-ness together with me from the beginning.)*

16:1 I have communicated these things to you so you will not be embarrassed about your scandalous association with me.

16:2 You will be kicked out of their synagogues and there will be times where those who kill you will think that they have done God a favor!

16:3 They will do these things because they know neither the Father nor me.

16:4 I have told you all this in advance so that when it happens you will remember this conversation. While I was with you there was no need for me to tell you about these things.

16:5 But now I am going away to be face to face with him who sent me! And here you are not even asking me to explain to you what I am about to do,

16:6 since you are so worried about your own future!

16:7 Now listen up! Hear me, my departure is not to disadvantage you; everything that is about to happen, brings conclusion and bears together what the Prophets pointed to! This will be to your absolute advantage! If I do not go away, your [1]Companion cannot come to you, but if I go I will send to you One to be [2]face to face with you defining your very being. (*[1]Parakletos, from para and kaleo; redefining our original being in the closest possible association and kindred companionship; closer to you than your breath! Again the word [2]pros is used!*)

16:8 In this capacity of close companionship with you, Holy Spirit comes to convince the world concerning sin, righteousness and judgment:

16:9 Holy Spirit in you will persuade them concerning their sin, which boils down to a bankrupt, distorted identity due to their indifference to me. (*The world's unbelief and indifference to Jesus is the very cause of their bankruptcy! The word for sin, [1]hamartia from ha, negative and meros, portion or form, thus to be without your allotted portion or without form, pointing to a disorientated, distorted or bankrupt identity; the word meros, is the stem of the word morphe, as in 2 Corinthians 3:18 where the word metamorphe, with form, [transform] is the opposite of hamartia - without form. Sin is to live out of context with the blueprint of one's design; to behave out of tune with God's original harmony.*)

116

16:10 In this union with you, the great Companion will also convince the world of righteousness because in my disappearing out of sight, to be face to face with the Father, the Spirit of truth will interpret the conclusion of my mission which is mankind's association in me and their redeemed innocence! The intimate union with my Father that I displayed while present with you in my physical body will now be made visible in you!

16:11 Then the world will be convinced that the judgment that was their due was accomplished when the ruler of this world system was judged. *(Just like Jesus and the Father - the Holy Spirit will not condemn the world but rather convince the world! In Jesus dying mankind's death, closure was brought to the system of the law of works and performance as dictating and defining human life. In mankind's co-crucifixion and joint-descent in Jesus into their hell and in their co-resurrection and co-elevation to be seated together with him in heavenly places! See John 5:21,22; John 12:31-33; Hosea 6:2, Ephesians 2:5,6; Colossians 3:1-3; Romans 4:25; Acts 17:29-31; 1 Peter 1:10,11; Hebrews 1:1-3.)*

16:12 I have so much more to tell you but you would not be able to handle it now.

16:13 But when she⑤is come, the Spirit of truth, she will④take you by the hand and guide you into the path of all truth. She will not draw attention to herself but will communicate and ①unveil everything she hears and discerns②from a heavenly perspective about the things that is④about to happen③within you. *(While spirit is in the neuter gender, truth is feminine. In Hebrew, the word for spirit is רוח ruach which is Feminine. The word ①οδηγησει, from odos, the pathway and hegeomai, the strengthened for of agoo, to lead, thus officially appointed Guide. The word ②anangellei, from ana, upward, above and angello, often translated angel; it has two components, ago to lead as a shepherd leads and agele a herd of cattle or company. The word ③umin, is the Personal Pronoun, you in the Dative case, also pointing to location "in." The things about to happen, ④erchomena, the Present Participle describes an action thought of as simultaneous with the action of the main verb. ⑤elthay, is come, When she, the Spirit of truth, is come [hotan elthēi ekeinos, to pneuma tēs alētheias]. Indefinite relative clause, hotan and the second Aorist Active subjunctive of erchomai, "whenever she comes." The Mood of the Greek verb, in this case the subjunctive, expresses the mode in which the idea of the verb is employed. See Hebrews 10:14,15 in the Mirror Bible.)*

RUACH is femenine (handwritten annotation above 16:13)

Notes on She - official appointed guide (handwritten annotation in right margin)

117

16:14 Holy Spirit will endorse my ¹opinion of you by taking that which is mine and ²interpreting it ³in you. *(The word often translated glory, ¹doxa from dokeo, to form an opinion. The word ²anangello, from ana, upward and angello to announce or declare. The preposition ana always points upward to the things that are above the earth's perspective. ³Umin, Personal Pronoun, you in the Dative case, also pointing to location "in.")*

16:15 The Father and I enjoy all things in common - even to the finest detail - because this is so, I said that the Close Companion esteems my glory and ²lays a hold of that which is within me and declares it within you from ¹heavens point of view. *(¹Ana, upward; The best texts read ²lambanei λαμβάνει, takes, instead of Λήψεται, lempsetai, shall take. The relation between the Son and the Spirit is present and constant. Vincent's Word Studies.)*

16:16 For a brief while I will be absent from your ¹view; then in another brief while you ²will see and know me. *(¹Ye shall not see - ou [negative] theorete - the present tense: "you behold me no more." - [theōreō - English, theorize] Then again you will ²see me, opsesthe, Future, middle Deponent Indicative of the verb horao. A different verb for seeing is used here. ¹Theoreo, emphasizes the act of vision, ²horao, the result. Theoreo a derivative of theaomai, denotes deliberate contemplation conjoined with mental or spiritual interest. "The vision of wondering contemplation, in which they observed little by little the outward manifestation of the Lord, was changed and transfigured into sight, horao, in which they seized at once, intuitively, all that Christ was. As long as his earthly presence was the object on which their eyes were fixed, their view was necessarily imperfect. His glorified presence showed him in his true nature." - Westcott.*

Paul beautifully prays that the eyes of our understanding be flooded with light so that we may know the full conclusion of his death and resurrection and how fully included we are in it.

The best texts omit, "Because I go unto the Father." Although it is present in the next verse.)

16:17 Some of his disciples said to each other, "What does he mean? He tells us that in a little while we won't see him. Then he tells us that in a little while we will see him again and then he would return to be face to face with the Father."

16:18 What does he mean by a little while? This just doesn't make sense to us at all.

16:19 Jesus perceived that they were confused about this and asked them, "Are you still trying to figure out what I mean by this brief time where you will no longer see me and then the next moment you will really see me?"

16:20 During this brief time of my apparent absence you will mourn and grieve but while the religious world rejoices, your pain will give birth to joy!

16:21 The anguish a woman suffers when her hour has come to give birth, is soon forgotten and replaced with delight when another [1]human life is born! (The word for the human species, male or female is [1]anthropos, from ana, upward, and tropos, manner of life; character; in like manner.)

16:22 Just like with childbirth where joy eclipses the labor pains, so your present sorrow will be vanquished and your hearts will erupt in joy when you realize how you captivate my [1]gaze! And no one will be able to take this joy away from you! (Again the word [1]οψομαι is used, from horaoo, to look at something with wide open eyes as in gazing at something remarkable! In the mirror reflection of his gaze, we see ourselves and now we know even as we have always been known!)

16:23 In that day of your awakening to our inseparable union, you shall ask me no more [1]questions; instead you should certainly [2]ask the Father directly in my name, knowing that my name represents the extent of all the Father has already accomplished on mankind's behalf and he will happily grant you your requests and take all questions of possible doubt or uncertainty out of the equation. (To question is the primary meaning of the verb [1]erotao. Another verb for ask occurs in the following sentence, [2]aiteo, to make a request.)

16:24 Until now you have not required anything in my name - when you realize what is yours in my name, then make your requests and lay a hold of that so that your joy may burst its banks!

16:25 I have used [1]examples to illustrate these things in figurative speech but the hour comes when the illustrations will be replaced with [2]unreserved utterance and I will [3]declare to you openly, heavenly things about the father. ([1]Paroimiais, from para and oiomai, to make like ("The kingdom of heaven is like a treasure hidden in an agricultural field..."), that is, imagine: - suppose, *think; parable or illustration. The word [2]parrhēsia, openly, frankly, without concealment. The word [3]anangello, from ana, upward and angello to announce or declare. The preposition ana always points upward to the things that are above the earth's perspective.)*

16:26 In that day you will make your [1]requests in my name without a middleman - there will be no need for me to [2]question the Father on your behalf. *(Again, as in verse 23, the words [1]aiteo, to make a request and [2]erotao, to question are used.)*

16:27 The Father himself is so fond of you and is pleased with your affection for me and your belief that I proceeded from his [1]immediate presence. *(The preposition [1]para, indicates close proximity, a thing proceeding from a sphere of influence, with a suggestion of union of place of residence, to have sprung from its author and giver, originating from, denoting the point from which an action originates, intimate connection.)*

16:28 I have indeed proceeded from the [1]immediate and intimate presence of the Father to come to the world and return again to be [2]face to face with the Father. *(Again John beautifully uses the words [1]para and [2]pros to communicate the level of intimacy within the Trinity.)*

16:29 The disciples said to him, "You are coming through loud and clear without the aid of a parable.

16:30   Now we see what you have seen all along! To be persuaded that you indeed proceeded from the Father brings an end to all our speculations and uncertainties!"

16:31 To this Jesus responded with, "Just when you think you now finally believe that I am who I claim to be,

16:32 then suddenly you will all scramble and run for your lives and abandon me! But I am never forsaken because my Father is always with me!

16:33 I have spoken these things to you that in me you will know the sweet and assured resonance of my peace! In the world you encounter extreme and stressful times, but be of good courage, [1]I have conquered the world-order!" *(Rev 3:21 And everyone's personal triumph will be celebrated together with me, by being jointly seated together in my Kingship! On exactly the same basis of [1]my victory celebration and my joint-seatedness with my Father in his throne! A.T. Roberston comments, [1]hōs kagō enikēsa is the first Aorist Active indicative of nikaō, to conquer; looking back* *on the victory as over in the past. In John 16:33 before the Cross Jesus says **egō nenikēka ton kosmon** which is in the Perfect Active tense, emphasizing the abiding effect of the victory! See Heb 1:3 Having made purification for sins, he sat down! His throne celebrates mankind's redeemed innocence!)*

17:1 Having said these things Jesus lifted up his eyes into the ¹heavenly sphere and spoke, "Father, the hour has come; this is the culmination of time! Glorify your Son; endorse your opinion of your Son so that the Son may mirror his opinion of you and cause your dignity and worth to be made renowned and rendered illustrious in order to become manifest and acknowledged throughout! *(The word ¹ouranos, heavenly sphere; from oros, mountain, from airō, to raise, elevate, to lift up. Here there exists no conflict of interest - only glory repeated in the other! And the glory of the Lord shall be revealed, and all flesh shall see it together! Isa 40:5.)*

17:2 Within the ¹mirror reflection of glory you co-²echo ³every nook and cranny of flesh on exhibit in the Son's ⁴authentic 'I-am-ness'! In order that every detailed aspect of what it takes to live life in the flesh may be be ⁵endued with the life of the ages. *(The word, ¹kathos, from kata, downward impression and hōs, as, like, even as, the same as; kathos follows on the previous thought of the co-exhibition of glory; the original image and likeness in the glory of the Father is again repeated and impressed in sonship. The word ²echo, to have in hand, to echo, resonate; the word ³pas, suggests each and every detail of all things; the whole, everyone, all things, everything. The word ⁴exousia, often translated authority, from ek, out of, source, and eimi, I am. The word ⁵didomi, to give, to endue, to return something to someone that already belongs to them. See John 1:14.)*

17:3 This life of the ages, invites them to engage in the ¹inexhaustible adventure of knowing you, the only true God and Jesus as the Christ whom you have commissioned! *(The word, ¹ginōskōsin, to learn to know, to perceive, to understand; in the Present Active Subjunctive form with hina [subject clause], "should keep on knowing.")*

17:4 I have caused your dignity and worth to be made renowned and rendered illustrious in order to become manifest and acknowledged throughout the earth by accomplishing the work which you have given me to do.

17:5 And now, oh Father, bestow the most intimate closeness of your own person upon me with the glory that I shared in your immediate presence even before the world was.

17:6 I have displayed your name and exactly who you are with distinction to those whom you have given me; they were yours in the first place then you gave them to me; they are also those who have treasured your word. *(Those who treasured the conclusion of your word, incarnate in me.)*

17:7 Now they too have come to know that everything you have given me originate in their own I-am-ness in you! *(Man began in God!)*

17:8 I have given them the very [1]words which you have given me in our conversation, which words they have embraced and have come to know that surely I also proceeded from you and are commissioned by you! *(Here the word rhemata [plural] is used and not logos like in verse 14 and most other references in John - rhema refers to the spoken word in conversation as such.)*

17:9 I pray specifically for them - those who know that they are yours to begin with and that you gave them to me. I'm not here to debate with those who still see themselves defined by the world-system!

17:10 I am greatly esteemed in our shared friendship with every individual person - all those who are mine are also yours and what is yours is mine.

17:11 I am no longer in the world but they are - I am proceeding to be face to face with you holy Father; I ask for the protection of those whom you have given me in your name that they also may be one even as we are.

17:12 While I was with them in the world I guarded over the ones you have given me in your name and did not [1]lose any, except the [1]lost son who fulfilled what was written prophetically. *(The word, ἀπώλεια [1]apōleia, which is often translated, perdition or destruction, has two components, apo, away from and ollumi, perish or lose, from luo, to loose. The same word, [1]apōleia, is used in Luke 15 - The shepherd did not "destroy" one sheep - he lost one sheep! Lost sheep, coin and son, all found, safe and sound! See my commentary note in John 6:71 on a most beautiful poem, written by my friend Dusty Harrison.)*

17:13 And now I come to be face to face with you Father; I speak these things while I am still in the world that they may have my joy fulfilled in themselves.

17:14 I have given them your Logos and now the world hates them because they have lost their manipulative, performance-based hold over them - these now know that they did not originate in the ¹cosmos but in the logos, even as I did not begin in the cosmos! *(The word ¹kosmos here refers to the natural order of things as evident in human tradition and philosophy.)*

17:15 I do not request that you take them out of the world but that you keep them from the ¹evil performance-based system of hardships, labors and annoyances! *(The ¹poneros-system is the system that is referenced in the Tree of the knowledge of good and evil (**poneros**) which is a system based on performance as the defining reference to human life - Jesus came to reveal and redeem our authentic value, identity and innocence as defining our lives.)*

17:16 They are not defined by the cosmos-system even as I am not defined thereby.

17:17 ¹Define them in your truth - your logos is the unveiled truth. *(The word ¹hagiazo speaks of a sanctification, a setting apart as in a defining moment.)*

17:18 Just as you have commissioned me into the world so I send them on their mission into the world!

17:19 For their sakes do I sanctify myself to be high above the cosmos-sytem so that their true set apart-ness *[from the performance based systems of the world]* will be mirrored in me.

17:20 I do not pray for them exclusively but also for those who would come to believe in me because of their word.

17:21 That they all may be one, exactly as you Father are mirrored in me and I in you, that they also will be exactly mirrored to be one in us - then the entire world will believe and be persuaded about your mission upon my life!

17:22 And I, *[the Incarnate word]* have endued them with the same glorious esteem that you have given me so that their oneness may mirror ours.

17:23 I am in them as you are in me, and on this basis their seamless oneness may be entirely concluded. Thus the world will acknowledge your commission upon my life and know that my love for them mirrors your love for me.

17:24 Father I desire that ¹what you have given me in them may cause them to be where I am so that they may see what I see and gaze attentively upon the splendor of my glory which you have given me *[in them]* because you loved me before the

²fall of the world. Thus the world will be persuaded that your love for them was never compromised because of the fall - you continued to love them the same! *(The best texts read, ¹ho not hous - that which. The word, ²kataballo, means "to fall away, to put in a lower place," instead of themelios, meaning "foundation" [see Ephesians 2:20]; thus, translated "the fall of the world," instead of "the foundation of the world." The entire "Fall" was a falling away in our minds from our true identity as image and likeness bearers of Elohim. Just like Eve, were we all deceived to believe a lie about ourselves, which is the fruit of the "I-am-not-tree ". We all, like sheep have gone astray. [Isa 53:6])*

17:25 Father of righteousness, while the world has not known you, I have known you and these here have come to know that you sent me.

17:26 And I have made the essence of your being known to them so that they may know you by name; and I will also give them understanding to know that the same love wherewith you have loved me is in them even as I am in them!

18:1 When Jesus concluded his prayer he and his disciples crossed over the brook Cedron into a garden.

18:2 Judas, who betrayed him was familiar with this place since Jesus often gathered there with his disciples.

18:3 Judas was given a Roman military cohort of about 600 soldiers to accompany him; they came together with temple officers from the chief priests and Pharisees with torches, lanterns and their weapons.

18:4 Jesus, fully aware of everything that was coming upon him, went forward to meet them and said, "Who are you seeking?"

18:5 They said to him, "Jesus the Nazarene." Jesus answered, "Here I am." And there Judas was, standing with them.

18:6 Just when Jesus said, "I am," they stumbled backwards and fell to the ground!

18:7 He asked them again, "Who are you looking for?" They said, "Jesus of Nazareth,"

18:8 Jesus said, "I already told you who I am; if its me you are after then let the others go."

18:9 He said this to confirm to his disciples that he would protect them so that none of them would be implicated.

18:10 Simon Peter thought that it was a good idea to defend themselves and drew his sword and struck at the high priest's servant, Malchus' head, who ducked away and lucky for him only lost an ear.

18:11 Jesus told Peter to put away the sword and said, "Do you think that I am not going to drink this cup the Father gave me?"

18:12 Then the soldiers under their captain's command together with the Jewish police arrested Jesus and tied him up.

18:13 They first took him to Annas, the father-in-law of Caiaphas who was the High Priest that year.

18:14 It was Caiaphas who advised the Jews that in order to save the entire nation, it was inevitable that one person should die.

18:15 Peter and another disciple followed Jesus; the High Priest knew the one disciple and he was allowed to enter the courtyard.

18:16 Peter remained outside at the entrance. Then the other disciple who knew the High Priest went to speak to the lady at the door and asked permission for Peter to join him inside.

18:17 The lady who guarded the door said to Peter, "Are you not also one of this man's disciples?" He said, "No I am not." *(She obviously recognized John as a disciple.)*

18:18 The slaves and temple police were huddled around a coal fire to warm themselves; Peter also joined them to get out of the cold.

18:19 The High Priest then began to question Jesus about his disciples and his teaching.

18:20 Jesus replied, "I have spoken openly to the world and frequently taught in the synagogues and temple to a Jewish audience and have said nothing in secret.

18:21 Why would you question me? Talk to my audience if you wish to find out about my teaching; they are familiar with what I teach."

18:22 When he said this one of the temple police slapped him in the face and scolded, "How dare you speak to the High Priest in this manner?"

18:23 Jesus answered, "If I said anything evil then tell me; but if I have spoken only that which is beautiful, why do you strike me?"

18:24 Annas sent him bound to Caiaphas, the High Priest. *(The proper place of this verse is immediately after the 13th.)*

18:25 In the mean time Peter was still warming himself at the fire when he was asked again if he was not one of the disciples of Jesus. He emphatically objected and said that he was not.

18:26 Then a relative of Malchus, whose ear Peter chopped off, also recognized him and said, "Did I not see you with him in the garden?"

18:27 Again Peter disclaimed it and just then, the cock crowed!

18:28 Then they led Jesus from Caiaphas into the praetorium, the Roman governor's judgment hall - it was still early in the day so the Jews didn't go into the court room for fear of contracting some impurity, which would have obliged them to separate themselves from eating the Passover.

18:29 Then Pilate went outside to face them and asked, "What accusation do you bring against this man?"

18:30 They answered, "If he wasn't an evildoer we wouldn't have wasted your time with this court case in the first place.

18:31 Then Pilate said, "Take him and judge him according to your law." They said, "Our law does not allow a death sentence."

18:32 This was also to confirm what Jesus said about his manner of death. *("I would be lifted up" - crucifixion was Roman and not a Jewish punishment; the Jews considered it a curse for a man to hang on a tree. 1 John 3:5 We have witnessed with our own eyes how, in the unveiling of the prophetic word, when he was lifted up upon the cross as the Lamb of God, he lifted up our sins and broke its dominion and rule over us! John 1:29 Behold, the Lamb of God, who takes away [airo] the sin of the world! The word airo means to lift up. John 3:14 (This is my mission: See the prophetic relevance - this is how the veil will be removed!) Remember how Moses lifted up the serpent in the wilderness even so the Son of man will be lifted up! See John 12:31 Now is the judgment of this world, now shall the ruler of this world be cast out; John 12:32 and I, when I am lifted up from the earth, will draw all judgment unto me. John 12:33 He said this to show by what death he was to die. John 3:13 and 14 are most significant since they point to the very essence of the mission of Jesus - the co-begotteness of the human race now redeemed in our co-crucifixion and co-resurrection on the third day into newness of life! 1 Peter 1:3. John 3:15 In the same prophetic pattern, I will be lifted up for all to see and be equally persuaded in the echo of the life of the ages now redeemed within them!)*

18:33 Than Pilate went back into the court room and summoned Jesus to him and asked him, "Are you the king of the Jews?"

18:34 Jesus responded, "Are these your own thoughts or did others suggest this about me?"

18:35 Pilate replied, "Am I a Jew, why would I bother to speculate about you? Your own people and priests handed you over to me. What have you done to make them do this?

18:36 Jesus answered, "My kingdom has nothing in common with the political or religious systems of this world; it does not originate out of their structures. If it did my subordinates would fight for me and resist my handover to the Jews."

18:37 Pilate then said, "So you are a king?" Jesus replied, "You say that I am a king. My destiny was to be born in the flesh and for this purpose have I come into the world to bear testimony to the truth. Everyone who recognizes their true origin, hears my voice." *(The truth about mankind's authentic sonship and the image and likeness of the invisible Father of the human race is evidenced in me and confirmed in my work of redeeming the human race from the futile ways they inherited from their fathers.)*

18:38 Pilate then asked him, "What is truth?" Without giving him a chance to respond, he went outside again to face the Sanhedrin and said to them, "I find no cause for any accusation in this man."

18:39 But since it is custom that I should release one of your prisoners during your festive time, would you be happy for me to pardon the King of the Jews for this Passover?"

18:40 They shouted back, "No, not this one, but Barabbas!" Barabbas was a Jewish freedom fighter, probably the leader of the band which included the other two who were crucified with Jesus.

19:1 Then Pilate took Jesus and gave order for him to be scourged. *(Scourging was the legal preliminary to crucifixion, but, in this case, was inflicted illegally before the sentence of crucifixion was pronounced, with a view of averting the extreme punishment, and of satisfying the Jews. The punishment was extreme, the victim being bound to a low pillar or stake, and beaten, either with rods, or, in the case of slaves and provincials, with scourges, called scorpions, leather thongs tipped with leaden balls or sharp spikes. The severity of the infliction in Jesus' case is evident from His inability to bear His cross. Vincent.)*

19:2 The soldiers plaited a crown of thorns and placed it on his head; they also threw a purple garment over him.

19:3 Then they positioned themselves in front of him and scorned him, saying, "Hail King of the Jews!" while continually slapping him in the face.

19:4 Then Pilate again went outside to the Sanhedrin saying, "Behold I am leading him out to you; I want you to know that I find no valid cause to condemn him."

19:5 Then Jesus came out of the Praetorium wearing a crown of thorns and the purple robe while Pilate announced, "Behold the man!" *(Idou ho anthrōpos; this exclamatory introduction of Jesus in mock coronation robes to the mob was clearly intended to excite pity and to show how absurd the charge of the Sanhedrin was that such a pitiable figure should be guilty of treason. Pilate failed utterly in this effort and did not dream that he was calling attention to the greatest figure of history, the Man of the ages. Robertson's word pictures.)*

19:6 When they saw him, the chief priests and the temple police shouted with rage, "Crucify! Crucify!" Pilate told them, "You take him and execute the crucifixion yourselves, I find no fault in him."

19:7 The Jews answered him, "We have our own law and by this law he must die because he made himself out to be the Son of God!" *(See John 5:18 This was fuel for the fire of Jewish zeal in their determination to execute Jesus! Not only did he break their Sabbath, but now he has gone beyond all extremes! He calls God his own Father - who does he think he is - God's equal?)*

19:8 The claim of Jesus' deity only served to accelerate Pilate's superstitious fears.

19:9 He went again into the judgment hall and asked Jesus, "Tell me, who are you really?" Jesus did not answer him.

19:10 Pilate said, "Why do you not answer me, do you not realize my position? I have the power to crucify or free you!"

19:11 Jesus said, "You have no authority over me, except what was given you from above. Therefore he *[Caiaphas, the High Priest]* who handed me over to you has the greater sin.

19:12 This motivated Pilate even more to make every effort to release him; but the Jews would not buy into it at all; they cried out, "If you even consider to release this man you prove that you are not loyal to Caesar - this man's claim to royalty makes him Caesar's enemy!"

19:13 These words persuaded Pilate to go through with the procedures. He led Jesus outside and sat down in judgment in a place called the Stone Pavement, a decorated mosaic area in the court which was called Gabbatha גבתא in Aramaic and Hebrew which means an elevated platform.

19:14 This was still during the preparation for the Passover, about the sixth hour. He announced to the Jews, "Behold! Your king!" *(About the sixth hour, ως εκτη **hōs hektē**. Roman time, about 6 a.m. when Pilate rendered his final decision. Mark 15:25 notes that it was the third hour ωρα τριτη **hōra tritē** (Jewish time), which is 9 a.m. Roman time, when the crucifixion began. Why should John give Jewish time writing at the close of the first century when Jerusalem and the Jewish state passed away in A.D. 70? Because he is writing for Greek as well as Roman readers. See also John 20:19.)*

19:15 But they cried out, "[1]Lift him up! Lift him up! Crucify him!" Pilate said, "Shall I crucify your king?" The Chief priests answered, "We have no other king but Caesar!" *(The word, [1]airo means to lift up, to elevate. See John 12:32,33.)*

19:16 He then handed Jesus over to them to be crucified and they led him away.

19:17 Bearing the cross himself, Jesus went out from the Courtyard to the place called Skull; its Hebrew name was Golgotha. *(גלגלת from גלל **galal** to roll away, as in Jos 5:9 And the LORD said to Joshua, "This day I have rolled away the reproach of Egypt from you." And so the name of that place is called Gilgal to this day.)*

19:18 There they crucified Jesus along with two others on either side of him.

19:19 Pilate wrote a placard and placed it on the cross. It read, "Jesus the Nazarene, the king of the Jews." *(Nazarite - "one separated" A name later given to Christians by the Jews, Acts 24:5.)*

19:20 Many of the Jews who came up to the Passover feast from other nations could read this title since the place where he was crucified was near the city and it was written in Hebrew, Latin and Greek.

19:21 But the Jewish rulers and priests complained about this and requested that he changes the wording to read, "He said, I am the king of the Jews."

19:22 To which Pilate replied, "What I have written, I have written!"

19:23 The soldiers who crucified Jesus took his outer garments and divided it between the four of them; the inner garment was a seamless woven tunic. *(The four pieces of the outer garment would be the head gear, the sandals, the girdle, the tallith which was the outer garment with fringes.)*

19:24 They therefore discussed between themselves to rather not tear the inner garment but to cast lots for it to determine whose it shall be. This was the fulfillment of prophetic Scripture, "They divided my outer garments among them and for my inner garment they cast lots." These very things predicted by David in Psalm 22:18, the soldiers unwittingly performed.

19:25 Standing by the cross were the three Mary's, the mother of Jesus, his aunt Mary the wife of Clopas and Mary of Magdala.

19:26 When Jesus saw his mother and the beloved disciple standing nearby, he said to her, "Ma'am, behold your son!"

19:27 Then he said to the disciple, "Behold your mother!" From that moment the disciple adopted her as his own mother. *(Westcott remarks upon the four exclamations in this chapter - Behold the man! Behold your King! Behold your son! Behold your mother! This gives us a remarkable picture of what Christ is, and what he reveals people to be.)*

19:28 With this Jesus, realizing that all things are now ¹**fully accomplished and that what was written was to be fulfilled, said, "I thirst!"** *(Everything is now done! Ede panta ¹tetelestai. Jesus studied Scripture with a different intent; he knew that he was reflected there! Familiar with the text, he brought context! Hebrews 10:7 "Then I said, I read in your book what you wrote about me; so here I am, I have come to fulfill my destiny." - Psalm 40:7, Luke 4:17, Luke 24:27, 44.)*

19:29 There was a jar filled with vinegar in which someone dipped a sponge attached to a branch of ¹**hyssop and lifted it to his mouth.** *(Compare these Scriptures, Matt 27:34; Psalm 69:21 They gave me gall for food, and for my thirst they gave me vinegar to drink. Also reference Deut 29:18; Jer 9:15; Jer 23:15; Lam 3:15; Lam 3:19; Amos 5:7; Amos 6:12. Hyssop was a reed used by the Hebrews in their ritual sprinklings.)*

19:30 When Jesus had taken the vinegar he said, "It is ¹**finished!" He then bowed his head and handed over the spirit.** *(See Psa 31:5 "Into Your hand I commit my spirit." The word ¹tetelestai communicates the final consummation of all things; everything is now concluded! John again - as in verse 28 - records this powerful word, in the Perfect Passive Tense which denotes an action which is completed in the past, but the effects of which are regarded as continuing into the present without end. Nothing that happens in time could possibly intercept this act of God's redemptive genius. The only possible way we can delay the glory that follows the cross is by underestimating what happened there when Jesus died and cried: "It is finished!" There is no eschatology of any one's guess or definition that carries more weight than God's 'eschatos' [final] word that he spoke to us in sonship - in the one who bears the very stamp [charakter] of his nature and radiates the Father's being. The one seated upon the throne of mankind's redeemed innocence! Heb 1:1-3 We can afford to make Jesus' words on the cross, "It is finished!" our complete and final focus! Charles Spurgeon said, in the word, tetelestai, we have an ocean of meaning in a drop of language!)*

19:31 The Jews were keen to have the bodies removed from the cross before sunset when the Sabbath began, especially since this particular Sabbath would coincide with the first day of unleavened bread which was a 'great' day. Their preparation for the feast of unleavened bread and eating the Passover meal was in full swing. They approached Pilate therefore and

requested that the bones of the victims be broken and that they might be lifted off the cross. *(To commemorate the unleavened bread that the Israelites ate when they left Egypt, they don't eat or even retain in their possession any "chametz" from midday of the day before Passover until the conclusion of the holiday. Chametz means leavened grain - any food or drink that contains even a trace of wheat, barley, rye, oats, spelt or their derivatives and wasn't guarded from leavening or fermentation. This includes bread, cake, cookies, cereal, pasta, and most alcoholic beverages. Ridding their homes of chametz is an intensive process. It involves a full-out spring-cleaning search-and-destroy mission during the weeks before Passover, and culminates with a search for chametz on the night before Passover, and then burning the chametz on the morning before the holiday.*

Instead of chametz, they eat matza - flat unleavened bread. It is a mitzvah to partake of matza on the two Seder Nights. During the rest of the holiday it is optional.

The highlight of Passover is the two "Seders," observed on the first two nights of the holiday. The first Seder is on Friday Evening, and the second Seder is on Saturday Evening. The Seder is a family oriented tradition and a ritual packed feast.

The focal points of the Seder are: Eating matza and bitter herbs to commemorate the bitter slavery endured by the Israelites. And drinking four cups of wine or grape juice - a royal drink to celebrate their newfound freedom.

The recitation of the Haggadah, a liturgy that describes in detail the story of the Exodus from Egypt. The Haggadah is the fulfillment of the biblical obligation to recount to our children the story of the Exodus on the night of Passover. See 1 Cor 5:6,7.)

19:32 The soldiers then broke the legs of the two men who were crucified with Jesus.

19:33 But when they saw that Jesus was already dead they did not break his legs.

19:34 One of the soldiers then pierced his side; blood and water flowed from the wound. *(The presence of these two elements was evidence that there had been heart rupture.)*

19:35 The one who witnessed these things has recorded their detail to convince the reader of their significance.

19:36 These things happened in fulfillment of that which was written prophetically, "No bone in the Pascal lamb shall be crushed." *(Ex 12:46 - 1500 - BC.)*

19:37 Also another Scripture which reads, "They shall gaze upon him whom they have pierced!" *(Zec 12:10.)*

19:38 Then Joseph of Arimathea asked Pilate permission to remove the body of Jesus which Pilate was pleased to do. Joseph was a prominent leader, and a secret follower of Jesus, *(but here, while most of his close friends and followers forsook him, Joseph fearlessly offers to bury Jesus in his own rock-hewn tomb! See Matthew 27:60 He was a rich man and a counsellor of the great Sanhedrin, Luke 23:50. Mark emphasizes the boldness of this act. Mark 15:43.)*

19:39 Also Nicodemus, who was the one who approached Jesus in the shelter of the night in order not to be publicly associated with him, made a very bold announcement of his love for Jesus and brought expensive sweet-smelling spices; a mixture of myrrh and aloes which weighed about a hundred pounds.

19:40 Then Joseph and Nicodemus took Jesus body and prepared it for burial. And according to Jewish custom they wrapped the body in linen cloths together with the spices.

19:41 In the area where he was crucified was a garden with a new tomb which was never used before.

19:42 Since it was still during their preparation for the Sabbath the location of the tomb where Joseph and Nicodemus placed Jesus, was conveniently close. *(The Hebrews reckoned two evenings, an earlier and a later. The former began midway between noon and sunset, or at three o'clock in the afternoon. The latter began at sunset, six o'clock. The reference here is to the earlier evening, though the time may have been well on toward the beginning of the later. The preparations had to be hurried because the Sabbath would begin at sunset - Vincent.)*

20:1 The first day of the Sabbaths, Maria from Magdala came to the tomb while it was still very early and saw that the stone was lifted out of the grave.

20:2 She left the tomb at once and ran to find Simon Peter and the other disciple whom Jesus was so fond of, and said to them, "They have taken the Lord out of the grave and we have no idea where they put him!" *(Mary fears a grave robbery. She did not suspect his resurrection.)*

20:3 So Peter and the other disciple immediately went to the tomb.

20:4 They were both running but the other brother out-ran Peter and arrived at the tomb first.

20:5 He stooped down and observed with careful attention the strips of linen cloth lying there, yet he did not enter. *(Seeing the grave cloths, he immediately knew that it wasn't a grave robbery!)*

20:6 Then Simon Peter also arrived and went straight into the tomb and took a long look at the grave cloths lying there.

20:7 He also noticed that the cloth that was wrapped around the head of Jesus, was not lying with the other strips of linen cloth, but neatly rolled up separately.

20:8 Then the other disciple who arrived there first also went in and he saw and was convinced! *(According to Luk 24:12 Peter went away "wondering" still.)*

20:9 It was as if they could not fully grasp that this was indeed what was predicted in Scripture, that Jesus was ¹destined to rise up out of death. *(See Psalm 16:10 "For you will not leave my soul in Sheol; you will not let your Holy One see corruption." Destined; must happen - ¹dei. See Mark 8:31; Matthew 26:54; Luke 9:22; Luke 17:25; Luke 22:37; Luke 24:7, Luke 24:26,27, Luke 24:44, 46; John 3:14; John 12:34; Acts 1:16. Jesus emphasized the fact and the necessity of his resurrection which the disciples slowly perceived.)*

20:10 The disciples went away to ¹face their own thoughts. *(¹pros hautous - facing themselves.)*

20:11 But Maria remained facing the tomb, weeping. Then she stooped down and ¹gazed into the tomb. *(The word, parakupto from para, close proximity and kupto to stoop down, bend forward, to view attentively with scrutiny.)*

136

20:12 She saw two celestial messengers, dressed in dazzling white and seated, one at the head and the other at the feet where Jesus' body had been lying.

20:13 They asked her, "Woman why are you weeping?" She said to them, "They took my Lord away and I do not know where they have put him."

20:14 As she said this she looked around [*as if she instinctively felt the presence of someone behind her*] and saw Jesus standing but did not immediately recognize him.

20:15 Jesus said to her, "Woman, why are you weeping? Who are you looking for? She thought he was the gardener and said, "Sir, if you have taken him away, please tell me where you put him so that I may fetch him!"

20:16 Jesus said to her, "Mariam!" she turned in her step and exclaimed, "Raboni!" which is Aramaic for, my Teacher! (*Also* רבוני *in Mark 10:5.1*)

20:17 "You'll have to let go of me, so that I may continue on to the Father. Go and tell my friends that I am ascending to my Father and your Father; to my God and your God!" (*She clung to him! [Like a bride to her husband!] Then Jesus said, mē mou haptou, present middle imperative in prohibition with the genitive case, meaning "no, do not cling to me!" She must have remembered his words in Jhn 16:4, "when it happens you will remember this conversation." Also, "it is to your advantage that I go!" See Luke 24:31 "And their eyes were opened and they recognized him; and he vanished from their sight." Instead of disappointment, a great excitement arrested their hearts and they took off in the night desiring to tell the others back in Jerusalem! They knew that Jesus could no longer be any more present in his person than what he is present in the Word incarnate in us!*)

20:18 So Maria the Magdalene went to the disciples and announced to them, "I saw the Lord!" And she told them all that he told her.

20:19 That evening of the first day of the week, the disciples were gathered in a room with the doors locked because they were afraid of the Jews. Suddenly Jesus stepped into their midst and said, "Shalom!" (*The addition of tēi miāi sabbatōn proves that John is using Roman time, not Jewish, for here evening follows day instead of preceding it. See John 9:14.*)

20:20 Then he showed them his scarred hands and side and having now seen the Lord for themselves, they were exceedingly glad!

20:21 Again he repeated his salutation and said, "Peace be unto you! Just as the Father has commissioned me so do I now send you!"

20:22 Having said this he [1]breathed an effusion of Spirit upon them and said, "[2]Take Holy Spirit as your Companion." *("Having breathed on them", [1]enephusēsen. First Aorist Active indicative of [1]emphusaō, late verb, here only in New Testament, though eleven times in the Septuagint and in the Papyri. From en, within, and phuo, to breathe, beget, bring forth, to spring up, to shoot forth. It was a symbolic act with the same word used in the Septuagint when God breathed the breath of life upon Adam (Gen 2:7). Jesus reminds his disciples of how his resurrection fulfilled the prophetic word in Hosea 6:2 and Ezek 37:1-9. The Valley of Dry Bones Ez 37:1 And the hand of the Lord came upon me, and the Lord brought me forth by the Spirit, and set me in the midst of the plain, and it was full of human bones. 2 And he led me round about them every way: and, behold, there were very many on the face of the plain, very dry. 3 And he said to me, Son of man, will these bones live? and I said, Oh Lord God, thou knowest this. 4 And he said to me, Prophesy upon these bones, and thou shall say to them, Ye dry bones, hear the word of the Lord. 5 Thus saith the Lord to these bones; Behold, I will bring upon you the breath of life: 6 and I will lay sinews upon you, and will bring up flesh upon you, and will spread skin upon you, and will put my Spirit into you, and ye shall live; and ye shall know that I am the Lord. 7 So I prophesied as the Lord commanded me: and it came to pass while I was prophesying, that, behold, there was a shaking, and the bones approached each one to his joint. 8 And I looked, and behold, sinews and flesh grew upon them, and skin came upon them above: but there was not breath in them. 9 And he said to me, Prophesy to the wind, prophesy, son of man, and say to the wind, Thus saith the Lord; Come from the four winds, and breathe [εμφυσησον emphuseson] upon these dead men, and let them live. Hebrew, nâphach נפח to kindle, inflate, breathe. Ez 37:10 So I prophesied as he commanded me, and the breath entered into them, and they lived, and stood upon their feet, a very great congregation.*

See John 7:37-39, Also John 14 and 16. The word [2]lambano, to take what is one's own, to take to one's self, to associate with one's self as Companion.

Holy Spirit seals and confirms our joint-resurrection with Jesus to be celebrated and endorsed in Feast of Pentecost.)

20:23 "If you ¹forgive someone's sins, they are ¹gone and forgotten. If you don't ²let go, then you are ²stuck with them." *(¹aphiēmi, to let go, to divorce, to leave behind, to forgive; ²krateō to seize. In the context of what has happened on the cross and here emphasized in the previous 3 verses, the basis of true forgiveness is the death and closure that Jesus brought to whatever it was that testified against us; his glorious resurrection and the companionship of Holy Spirit as the very breath of our zoe-life are the essence and authority of our commission which is to announce mankind's redeemed innocence!)*

20:24 But Thomas, the Twin, one of the Twelve, was not with them when Jesus came.

20:25 The other disciples told him that they have seen the Lord. But his response was, "I will never believe it unless I see his nail pierced hands and thrust my finger into the wounds and also my hand into his side."

20:26 The next Sunday evening, Jesus again just showed up in their midst even though all the doors were locked and greeted them with, "Peace be unto you!" This time Thomas was with them.

20:27 Jesus immediately turned to Thomas and said to him, "Give me your finger and touch my hands so you that can see for yourself; and give me your hand and thrust it into my side! Replace your scepticism with persuasion!"

20:28 Without hesitation Thomas responded to Jesus with, "My Lord and my God!"

20:29 Jesus said to him, "You believe because you saw with your own eyes; blessed are those who believe even though they do not see!"

20:30 The disciples of Jesus witnessed many more signs than the ones recorded in this book.

20:31 But what is written here is enough evidence for the reader to be absolutely convinced that Jesus is the Christ, the Son of God. And thus your belief will echo the zoe-life unveiled in his name.

21:1 Jesus also appeared to the disciples at the sea of Tiberias in the following incident:

21:2 Simon Peter and Thomas the twin, Nathaniel from Cana in Galilee, the Zebedee brothers and two of the other disciples were together.

21:3 It was Simon's idea to go fishing, so they joined him and got into a boat and spent the night trying, but caught nothing.

21:4 By daybreak Jesus was waiting for them at the shore but they did not recognize him.

21:5 Jesus asked them, "Lads, haven't you got anything to eat?" They said, "Nope!"

21:6 Then he told them to cast the net on the right side of the boat and they will definitely find some; so they did and took so many fish that they were unable to haul them in.

21:7 Then the disciple whom Jesus was so fond of said to Peter, "It is the Lord!" When Simon Peter heard that it was the Lord, he girded his outer garment around him since he was naked, and promptly jumped into the water.

21:8 The other disciples dragged the net full of fish with a little boat. They were only about 100 yards from the shore.

21:9 When they got out of the boat they were surprised to see a coal fire with fried fish and bread on it.

21:10 Jesus suggested that they also bring some of the fish they had just caught.

21:11 Simon Peter joined them and pulled the net ashore; they counted 153 large fish, and the net didn't even tear!

21:12 Jesus then invited them to break their fast and feast together. By now they knew beyond doubt that it was the Lord and didn't even bother to ask him.

21:13 Jesus took the bead and handed it to them and also the fish.

21:14 This was the third time Jesus appeared to the disciples since he rose from the dead.

21:15 After they had their breakfast Jesus asked Simon Peter, "Simon of Jonah, do you agape me more than any of the others?" He answered, "Surely Lord, you see how fond I am of you!" He said to him, "Show your love for me by feeding my little lambs." *(Note the use of agapao and phileo in this conversation.)*

21:16 He asked a second time, "Simon of Jonah, do you agape me?" He answered, "Of course Lord, you know that you are my best friend." He said, "Then shepherd my sheep."

21:17 He asked him a third time, "Simon of Jonah, are you very fond of me?" By now Peter was feeling a little uncomfortable that Jesus asked him a third time, "Do you dearly love me?" He answered him, "Lord I cannot hide anything from you, and you know very well how fond I am of you!" And Jesus said to him, "Then nourish my sheep."

21:18 "You can mark my words, when you were younger you could choose what you wanted to wear and moved about freely wherever you wished; but there will come a time when someone else will dress you and take you where you do not want to go."

21:19 He pointed prophetically to Peter's martyrdom and death by which he would glorify God. And Jesus said to him, "Follow me."

21:20 Peter turned around and saw Jesus' beloved disciple following them; he was also the one who would lean against the chest of Jesus at the dinner table and asked, "Lord who will betray you?"

21:21 Seeing him Peter asked, "Lord, what about this man?"

21:22 Jesus said to him, "If I would rather have him remain while I am ¹going, should not concern you; just keep close company with me. *(The word ¹erchomai can mean coming or going - depends on the context.)*

21:23 So a rumor began amongst the followers that this disciple would not die. Yet Jesus didn't say that he wasn't going to die, he said, "If I wish that he remains while I am going should not concern you."

21:24 This is the very disciple who is bearing witness to all these things in this writing. We confirm that his testimony is true.

21:25 Were the vastness of the work and words of Jesus carefully detailed, the libraries of the world could not contain them. *(See John 20:30.)*

In this final chapter and Epilogue to his book, John beautifully highlights a significant parallel, reflecting on their first encounter with Jesus, when, as business partners he and his brother James and Simon Peter toiled all night and had nothing to show for their efforts; here he portrays Peter taking the initiative to go back fishing to possibly help them deal with the extreme emotional tensions of the past days and also his disappointment with himself in denying Jesus three times. In John's account, Jesus again demonstrates dramatically how a greater grace dimension that outperforms their best efforts and intentions, eclipses their familiar world with its highs and lows. In Jesus' conversation with Peter, as Simon the son of Jonah, he deliberately calls him this name again to remind him of the significant moment when he discovered by revelation that in Jesus as the son of man, our physical identity is surpassed by a greater identity and birth, we are hewn out of the same rock; we share sonship because we have the same Father! This is the foundation of the ekklesia that Jesus builds. [Matthew 16.] Then instead of blaming Peter for denying him, Jesus deliberately reminds him of their friendship where their love for one another is reinforced three times; this love union will also be the basis of Peter's role in his shepherd leadership of Jesus' flock. It is also interesting to note the names of Thomas, and Nathaniel in the account of the fishing episode; they, too, had their moments of doubt.

Lydia and Francois met on the 25th of August 1974, while he was working with Youth For Christ. She was sixteen and he nineteen! The following year he studied Greek and Hebrew at the University of Pretoria for three years while Lydia completed her nursing training. In 1978 Francois also spent a year with Youth with a Mission. They married in January 1979 and are blessed with four amazing children, Renaldo, Tehilla, Christo and Stefan; also, two darling grandchildren Nicola and Christiaan.

They worked in a full-time mission for fourteen years, during which time they also pastored a church and led a training facility for more than 700 students over a five-year period. They then left the ministry and for ten years did business mainly in the tourism industry. They built and managed a Safari Lodge in the Sabi Sand Game Reserve and eventually relocated to Hermanus where they started Southern Right Charters boat-based whale watching.

In December 2000 Francois began to write the book, "God believes in You" which led to him being invited to speak at various Christian camps and churches. Since February 2004, they travelled regularly abroad and into Africa as well as South Africa.

Francois has written several books in both English and Afrikaans, including God Believes in You, Divine Embrace, The Logic of His Love and The Eagle Story; these are also available on Kindle. Also Kant En Klaar [Done!]

In order to focus their time on writing and translation, they relocated from Hermanus in 2015 to a remote farm in the Swartberg Mountains. They have also stopped most of their travelling.

Lydia has written 6 amazing children's stories of which Stella's Secret, The Little Bear And The Mirror, Kaa of the Great Kalahari as well as The Eagle Story, are already published in print and on Kindle. Her most recent story "King Solitaire's Banquet" will be released soon.

Francois continues to be passionately engaged in his translation of the Mirror Bible, which will eventually include the entire NT as well as select portions of the old. The 1st 250 page A5 Edition was published in 2012.

Lydia's books are already available in English Afrikaans, German and Spanish.

The Mirror Bible is currently available in Spanish, Shona, Xhosa and large portions in German.

Thousands of people subscribe to their daily posts on Social Media; Lydia has her own fb page and Francois has 5 English pages on Facebook.

You can get more detail about them on **www.mirrorword.net**

The Mirror Bible is also on Kindle as well as an App, **app.mirrorword.net**

REFERENCES and RESOURCES

Referred to by the author's name or by some abridgement of the title.

Adam Clarke (1762–1832 A British Methodist theologian)

Ackerman *[Christian Element in Plato]*

Bruce Metzger *(Textual Commentary on the Greek NT)*

Barnes Notes (Notes on the Bible, by Albert Barnes, [1834], at sacred-texts. com)

BBE (1949, Bible in Basic English)

Doddrich (Philip Doddridge 1702-1751 www.ccel.org/d/doddridge)

Dr. Robinson (Greek Lexicon by Edward Robinson1851)

E-Sword by Rick Meyers (www.e-sword.net)

J.H. Thayer (Greek-English Lexicon of the New Teatament By Joseph Henry Thayer, DD - Edinburgh - T&T CLARK - Fourth Edition 1901)

J.B. Phillips Translation (Geoffrey Bles London 1960)

Jeff Benner http://www.ancient-hebrew.org/

KJV (King James Version - In 1604, King James I of England authorized that a new translation of the Bible into English. It was finished in 1611)

Knox Translation (Translated from the Vulgate Latin by Ronald Knox Published in London by Burns Oates and Washbourne Ltd. 1945)

Marvin R. Vincent (1834-1922) Word Studies.

NEB (New English Bible New Testament - Oxford & Cambridge University Press 1961)

Robert Charles *R. H. (Robert Henry), 1855-1931*

RSV (The Revised Standard Version is an authorized revision of the American Standard Version, published in 1901, which was a revision of the King James Version, published in 1611.)

Strongs (James Strong - Dictionary of the Bible)

The Message (Eugene H. Peterson Nav Press Publishing Group)

Walter Bauer (Greek English Lexicon - a translation of Walter Bauer's Griechisch-Deutches Worterbuch by Arndt and Gingrich 1958)

Wesley J. Perschbacher (The New Analytical Greek Lexicon Copyright 1990 by Hendrickson Publishers, Inc)

Westcott and Hort *The New Testament in the Original Greek 1881*

Weymouth New Testament *(M.A., D.Lit. 1822-1902)*

Zodhiates Complete Word Study Lexicon Mantis Bible Study for Apple